D1295235

This magnificent new book, *31 Decrees of Blessing for Women*, by Patricia King, will empower believers with the tools to boldly release decrees that will unlock the blessings of heaven, align hearts with the Word of God, and bring change to their lives. Bravo!

—Jane Hamon, Vision Church @ Christian International

Patricia King has found the keys to releasing the blessing of the Father through the spoken Word to create supernatural breakthroughs in the name of Jesus and by the power of the Spirit. Whenever we put application to the revelation of the Word by scriptural decrees, miracles happen! Get ready for the most dramatic answers to prayer ever!

—Pastor Tony Kemp, president, the ACTS Group

Read *31 Decrees of Blessing for Women* and be edified, empowered, and blessed.

—Joan Hunter, author and healing evangelist

Patricia King has been the voice in my life who always points me like a compass toward Christ. There have been times during my journey with the Lord that I wrestled with not knowing who I was in Him. Yet through Patricia's godly counsel and wisdom from Scripture, she helped me discover my identity as a servant, revivalist, leader, and a woman. No matter what issue I have struggled with, her timely biblical insight assisted me in working successfully through those things that were hampering my growth and victory. In this book, Patricia has fashioned these powerful decrees to do the same for you too. Read *31 Decrees of Blessing for Women* and get ready for your breakthrough!

—Katie Souza, Katie Souza Ministries

Patricia King's new book, *31 Decrees of Blessing for Women*, is sure to jump-start your faith, revive your heart, and set you on a pathway of personal victory. Patricia dives deep into the Word in every daily devotion as she shares personal stories of breakthrough. Each devotion is followed by ten decrees—straight from Scripture. I want to encourage you to say these decrees out loud. Sing them out and write them down. Put them in your car, in your purse, on your phone or iPad, or in your kitchen for each day. I have watched Patricia's life flourish in God and in ministry as she has become a fearless leader in the body of Christ. She has always taken the Word, believed the Word, and decreed the Word out loud. Now she is sharing these powerful testimonies and decrees with us. Let's take the Word, decree it, and watch God move. Let's become fearless women of God.

—Julie Meyer, author of *Singing the Scriptures*, Intotheriver.net

I used to *not* believe that prophetic decrees were powerful. *Until* I began to listen closely to what Patricia King was teaching and is teaching in this book. Decrees, when done in true faith and with true need, are explosively powerful. But don't take my word for it. Get *31 Decrees of Blessing for Women* for yourself and a friend. Powerful!

—Steve Shultz, founder, The Elijah List and Elijah Streams TV

In every generation the Lord raises up forerunners and eventually champions over an arena of truth. Patricia King is both a relentless forerunner for the things of the Lord, and she has also emerged as a champion, composing decrees that lead the way in this generation. It is an extreme honor to add my blessing to this devotional book on decreeing a blessing, especially designed for today's women. Thank you, Patricia!

—Dr. James W Goll, founder of God Encounters Ministries, GOLL Ideation LLC

31 Decrees
OF
Blessing

FOR WOMEN

By Patricia King

BroadStreet
PUBLISHING

BroadStreet Publishing® Group, LLC
Savage, Minnesota, USA
BroadStreetPublishing.com

31 DECREES OF BLESSING FOR WOMEN

Stock or custom editions of BroadStreet Publishing titles may be purchased in bulk for educational, business, ministry, fundraising, or sales promotional use. For information, please email info@broadstreetpublishing.com.

Cover design by Chris Garborg at garborgdesign.com
Typesetting by Kjell Garborg at garborgdesign.com

Printed in China
19 20 21 22 23 5 4 3 2 1

CONTENTS

INTRODUCTION

As a woman who loves the Lord, the proclamation of decrees based on Scripture has revolutionized my life, family, relationships, and ministry. I have experienced increase and multiplication of blessings in every area of my life since I began to regularly decree positive, faith-filled words of truth. As a leader and mentor of women, I have shared with many this treasured tool for success and have discovered the effect and influence of God's goodness on their lives to be remarkable.

The word *decree* is a legal term that means:

1. An official order given by a person with power or by a government
2. An official decision made by a court of law[1]

The words we speak have power and can potentially create life or death (James 3:5–10), but when we make a legal proclamation that comes from God Himself, we are then operating in a power that trumps all other power.

Jesus said, "The words that I speak unto you, *they* are spirit, and *they* are life" (John 6:63 KJV). His words are filled with power and have the ability to create His kingdom's glory on the earth. When you proclaim God's Word in faith, it is activated to bring about His will and purpose for your life.

Examine the following encouraging Scripture from the Amplified Bible to see how powerful His Word is: "For the word of God is living and active and full of power [making it operative, energizing, and effective]" (Hebrews 4:12 AMP).

When you decree God's Word, it is alive and full of power and brings itself to pass. According to Isaiah 55:11, it does not return empty but accomplishes everything it is sent to do. God's Word is the final authority. If He said it, He will make it good!

In the book of Job, we find this profound and powerful statement: "Decree a thing, and it will be established" (Job 22:28

NASB). In Esther 8:8, we discover further confirmation: "A decree which is written in the name of the king and sealed with the king's signet ring may not be revoked" (NASB).

Jesus, our eternal King, has given us all the glorious promises in the Word. They are for every child of God to enjoy. When you decree these blessings in faith, they will come to pass. It is like building a framework in the spirit realm that the power of God then fills with manifestation of the promise. The word you decree attracts the manifestation of what has been proclaimed. Every word you decree has power.

This book is especially designed to inspire women with a daily devotion, based on life-giving Scriptures in The Passion Translation for every day of the month, that will turn your attention to the heart of God and His wonderful intentions for your life. Each devotion is followed by ten powerful decrees that are based on the Word of God. Scripture references are also available for you at the bottom of each page of decrees, to read individually if you desire. This will help you receive the full impact from them as you meditate on the truth they contain, allowing them to renew your mind. Finally, there is a daily activation for you in response to each devotion and the corresponding decrees. Acting on the Word of God helps seals it in your heart and life.

There is a devotion, decree, and activation for every day of a month. As you use this devotional, watch your confidence and spiritual empowerment grow. Transformation is sure to take place as you daily give Him your focus. Use this book to bless every aspect of your life.

Here are some benefits that await you as you give God's Word your focus:

1. The Word you meditate on and decree will not return void but will accomplish everything it is sent to do (Isaiah 55:11).

2. Your decrees of the Word will frame the will of God over your life, allowing the Spirit to fill the framework and manifest results (Hebrews 11:3).

3. The Word you proclaim will dispatch angels to labor on your behalf as you become God's voice for His Word to be released on the earth (Psalm 103:20).

4. Your decrees of the Word will send forth light that will penetrate darkness (Psalm 119:130).

5. Blessings will be attracted to you as you proclaim in faith the promises He has given you as a believer.

6. You will create in your life and on the earth what was not present previously, through faith-filled decrees (Romans 4:17).

7. The Word proclaimed functions as a weapon of spiritual warfare and secures victory for your life (Ephesians 6:10–20; 2 Corinthians 10:3–5).

8. Your decrees of God's Word will empower and strengthen you in your innermost being (Ephesians 3:16).

9. The Word decreed is like seed that goes forth and brings a harvest for you according to the nature of the seed (Mark 4:3–20).

10. Sanctification (setting you apart for God and His purposes) is activated through the proclamation of God's truth declared over your life (John 17:17).

My prayer as you walk through this thirty-one day devotional of decrees is that your life will be enriched and blessed beyond measure. May God's blessings truly come upon you and overtake every area of your life (Deuteronomy 28:2).

BLESSED WITH INSPIRED WORDS FROM GOD'S HEART

King Lemuel's royal words of wisdom:
These are the inspired words my mother taught me.

PROVERBS 31:1

When God created woman, He gave her His maternal nature and instincts. Every person He has created, male or female, has a place that needs to be filled with His motherly nurture. King Lemuel (King Solomon)[2] took to heart the inspired words of his mother. Her words made a huge impact on him—so much so that an entire chapter of the Bible is dedicated to those memorable, inspired words.

All of us have or had a mother. Perhaps she was absent in your life or not able to give you the nurture and care you needed, but we all are here because we had a mother—the person who gave us life.

We know very little about David's upbringing, but we do see in the Word that he wasn't regarded highly in his family. When all his brothers were lined up for Samuel to select one to be king, David wasn't even considered; and when Samuel asked if there were any more sons, David's family hesitated and made reference to his lack of value in their eyes by sharing that he was simply the youngest who was out tending the sheep. David also alluded to his parents' role in his life in Psalm 27:10: "My father and mother abandoned me. I'm like an orphan! But you took me in and made me yours."

Every child needs to be celebrated, accepted, nurtured, and loved, but in David's case, it was God Himself who met those needs in his life due to his parents' shortcomings. Both natures—those of a mother and father—are within God.

Like with David, God wants to meet your needs too. Perhaps you understand the rejection or lack of worth David must have felt (whether it was a member of your family who rejected you or someone else close to you). No matter what your natural mother was like, or what kind of motherly examples you received in your school years and in church, as well as other motherly figures you had in your life at various times, God is there to make up for any gap you may have experienced.

If you think back through your life, you will discover that God was there to send inspired words that flowed from His maternal nature and care for you. Perhaps you can remember words that your grandmother, mother, aunt, friends, acquaintances, or spiritual leaders spoke into your life that made an impact. God was using them to speak life-giving maternal words of wisdom to you. Those are the words you will remember, just like Solomon remembered the words of wisdom from God's heart, spoken through his mother. They made a lasting impact on his life.

God is raising up many women in the body of Christ today to nurture His people spiritually. For individuals who did not receive His maternal nurture through a natural mother, He is raising up spiritual mothers, anointed of Him, who will give His children what they need.

As a woman, you need God's maternal input and encouragement, but you also have the capacity in Christ to give His nurture to others. He is calling His women to rise up and represent His nature and wisdom to those who will grow up into His calling and destiny. I believe He is calling you.

DECREES

I DECREE THAT:

1. I am a recipient of God's inspired words and Spirit that grant me His maternal nurture, love, and care.

2. I am filled with this love and nurture, and nothing whatsoever will ever separate me from the love God has poured upon me.

3. God's maternal love for me never fails; it is rich and forgiving, so gentle and kind.

4. God's maternal love is over me as a banner that gives me covering and victory, leading me in the way I should go.

5. I follow after God because He draws me with His intimate maternal and nurturing love.

6. I have been called to know God's maternal care and His rich love that surpasses knowledge so that I am filled with His fullness.

7. I truly am the object of God's deepest love and affection.

8. Because of His love for me, I will never perish but will have everlasting life with Him and am able to impart that love and life to others.

9. The love of God wells up within me like fresh rain from above and overflows me with perfect peace, wisdom, and insights that I can share with others.

10. The Lord pours His unfailing love upon me daily, and as a result, I am able to love others freely, inspiring them in His love.

Decrees based on the following Scriptures: Proverbs 31:1; Jeremiah 31:3; 1 John 3:1; Romans 8:38–39; 1 Corinthians 13:4, 7–8; Song of Solomon 1:2, 4; 2:4; Ephesians 3:18–20; John 3:16; Psalm 42:8; Luke 6:35.

ACTIVATION

Take some time to be alone with God and ask Him to remind you of key inspired words that have been spoken into your life by those who represent His maternal heart. Write them out and meditate on them. Throughout the week, add more to the list as you remember them.

Consider sending a thank-you note to those who have impacted your life with their inspired words.

_____

_____

_____

_____

_____

_____

_____

_____

_____

_____

DAY TWO

BLESSED WITH RADIANT BEAUTY

*For your royal Bridegroom is ravished
by your beautiful brightness.*

PSALM 45:11

I remember meeting a group of teenage girls in a sauna at the public pool just before I received the Lord. I was in a very dark place in my life at the time, but when I looked at them I could not get over their beauty. They radiated a brightness that I had not seen before, and it made me wonder what the source of this radiance was. I listened carefully, attempting to discover a clue as they shared with each other, but they were just being normal teenagers—nothing spiritual or profound was being communicated.

I finally asked them, "Where are you from?" They shared that they were from a church in the city and were enjoying a youth night together. I was so captured by this radiant beauty they exuded that I felt prompted to consider finding a church to attend. Just a few weeks later, I received Jesus as my personal Savior, and my life has been transformed since that time. Their light drew me to Christ.

As believers, we don't necessarily see our own radiance in Christ. When we get up in the morning and look at our "morning face" in the mirror, we are not usually gazing at the glorious beauty of Christ manifested on our face, and yet His glory and radiance are within us; they are always there—morning, noon, and night. Those in darkness behold that beauty and light, taking note of it even when we don't.

I saw the light on those girls, and I knew it was not natural—it was something greater than them, for sure. The girls, however, were most likely not aware of their "glow" at all.

Jesus is always beholding your glory and radiance. He can't stop thinking about you. He is ravished by your beauty and brightness, and His desire is that you will see His beauty in yourself.

All of us at times may feel a bit frumpy, disheveled, and missing the mark of beautiful outward appearance, but God wants us to see beyond the outer layer. He looks at the heart. He sees your beauty and radiance. "God sees not as man sees, for man looks at the outward appearance, but the Lord looks at the heart" (1 Samuel 16:7 NASB).

Jesus said in John 10:10, "A thief has only one thing in mind—he wants to steal, slaughter, and destroy." The devil would love to steal the truth about your beauty from you. He is a liar, a killer, and a thief. Any time you receive adverse thoughts about your beauty and loveliness, you need to call the devil a liar and believe the exact opposite.

The Word reveals who you truly are. God says you are beautiful. He says you are lovely and radiant, and He is God and cannot lie. He has given you the blessing of radiant beauty. Look for that beauty in yourself. Believe in that beauty. Focus on that beauty—and then go into the world and let that beauty shine.

Her shining light will not be extinguished,

no matter how dark the night.

Proverbs 31:18

DECREES

I DECREE THAT:

1. I am truly blessed with beautiful brightness in Christ.
2. Christ in me is my hope of glory. He is the glory and the lifter of my head.
3. I shine as a light in the world I live in.
4. The Lord delights in me.
5. The beauty of the Lord is upon me as I go about my day.
6. I arise and shine, for my light has come and the Lord's glory appears upon me.
7. His radiance in me is like the sunshine.
8. The Lord makes His face shine upon me and is gracious to me.
9. The Lord has crowned me with glory and majesty.
10. My radiant beauty is ever renewed within me.

Decrees based on the following Scriptures: Psalm 45:11; Colossians 1:27; Psalm 3:3; Matthew 5:16; Song of Solomon 7:6; Psalm 90:17; Isaiah 60:1–3; Habakkuk 3:4; Numbers 6:25; Psalm 8:5; Job 29:20.

ACTIVATION

Look in the mirror. Do you see the beauty and radiance that God has given you? You are altogether lovely. Meditate on God's glorious light within until you are able to embrace the truth of that revelation. Then go about your day releasing that radiance.

_____

_____

_____

_____

_____

_____

_____

_____

_____

_____

_____

_____

DAY THREE

BLESSED WITH POWER

She wraps herself in strength,
might, and power in all her works.
PROVERBS 31:17

Are you filled to overflowing with the power of the Holy Spirit? Is His presence and power influencing the world through you? When the power of the Holy Spirit flows through us, light invades the darkness and the world is transformed. The word *power*, used by Jesus in Acts 1:8, is a Greek word, *dynamis*³ (some use *dunamis*). It is the power that enables you to work miracles, to be strengthened, to obtain wealth, to win battles, and to be of excellent character. This power is available to you if you are a believer. You can change your life when you exercise this power. You cannot simply lean on your own understanding; you must exercise God's power.

Jesus taught in John 7 that out of your innermost being the Spirit and His power would flow: "'Believe in me so that rivers of living water will burst out from within you, flowing from your innermost being, just like the Scripture says!' Jesus was prophesying about the Holy Spirit that believers were prepared to receive" (vv. 38–39).

Maria Woodworth Etter (1844–1924) was a famous tent revivalist who allowed the power of God to flow through her mightily. Many would flood her tent meetings believing they would experience God's power. Those who attended these meetings testified of the tangible presence and miracle-working grace of God's Spirit. There was so much manifest power in her meetings that the convicting presence of the Holy Spirit would inundate the streets of the cities she ministered in, and as a result, many would cry out to be saved. She was a woman known to this day for boldly operating with uncompromised faith in God's miracles, signs, and wonders.

On the day of Pentecost, the Holy Spirit and His power filled everyone who was in the upper room, including the women. The outpouring did not remain in the upper room but filled the streets, and three thousand were added to the church the first day.

Peter explained the outpouring by referring to Joel's prophecy: "This is what I will do in the last days—I will pour out my Spirit on everybody and cause your sons and daughters to prophesy. ... The Holy Spirit will come upon all my servants, men and women alike" (Acts 2:17–18). This was the outpouring of power Jesus had spoken to them about. It is important that we embrace and steward the power that has been entrusted to us.

God is raising up a great company of women who are powerful in Him. They are preaching the gospel, prophesying, working miracles, healing the sick, raising the dead, setting captives free, and confronting injustice. They are a powerful company, and you are invited to be part of that company. God has His hand on you! This creative, awesome power can be released in your home, your workplace, the marketplace, and on the streets.

Wherever you are, God's power can be ministered because His power is in you; you just have to let it out.

DECREES

I DECREE THAT:

1. God's power fills me to overflowing by His Holy Spirit.
2. I can do all things through Christ who empowers me.
3. God's power is upon my life and activated to bless the world around me.
4. I have moral excellence due to God's power living within me.
5. I have the power to work miracles in Christ as I activate them through faith and obedience to the Spirit.
6. I have the power to obtain wealth.
7. The sick are healed by the power of Christ when I lay hands on them.
8. In Christ's power and name, I cast out demons.
9. Through Christ, I have power over the enemy and nothing will injure me.
10. I preach the gospel boldly through the power of the Spirit.

Decrees based on the following Scriptures: Acts 1:5, 8; Philippians 4:13; Deuteronomy 8:18; Mark 16:17–18; Luke 10:19.

ACTIVATION

Take time today to ask God to fill you afresh with His Holy Spirit's power. Invite His power to strengthen you, fill you with excellence of soul, empower you to create wealth, win any battle you are facing, and believe God for a miracle where you see the need. Praise Him for His power.

_____

_____

_____

_____

_____

_____

_____

_____

_____

_____

_____

DAY FOUR

BLESSED WITH FAVOR

Gabriel appeared to her and said,
"Grace to you, young woman, for the Lord is with you
and so you are anointed with great favor."
LUKE 1:28

Mary was a young woman when she was called to a supreme assignment: to give birth to Jesus Christ, the Messiah. From an earthly perspective, she did not have many qualifications for this enormous task, but she had God's favor that enabled her to accomplish it.

When you are a believer in Jesus, you too have the blessing of this great favor available to you: "the Lord is with you and so you are anointed with great favor." It is a gift from God and cannot be earned. This is wonderful news. Four definitions of *favor*[4] are:

1. To be approved of or liked

When God's gift of favor is at work in your life, you will have approval in the eyes of others. Sometimes you cannot explain why you are receiving such favor. That's because it is a gift. This is one way God's favor is activated in your life. We see an example of this in the life of Esther. The king favored her more than all the other women for no apparent reason, and as a result of his approval, she was able to bring deliverance to her nation after she became his queen.

2. To be given privilege and preferential treatment

When you are favored, you are granted privilege and special treatment. Joseph was favored in Potiphar's house, and although he was bought as a slave, he lived like the master of the house. Even when he was in prison, he was not treated like a prisoner. The chief jailer gave him special treatment and privileges. This is God's blessing of favor.

3. To be given benefits and gifts

When you are favored, gifts and benefits will come to your life. In Psalm 45:11–12, we discover that gifts shower the one whom the Bridegroom loves. That's you! Often I am lavished with beautiful gifts and benefits that I do not deserve. It is God's favor simply because I am His beloved. You can expect this blessing of favor when you love Jesus.

4. To be given unfair advantage

When you are favored, you are often granted advantage that you never earned or deserved. Years ago, on the mission field in Tijuana, Mexico, we needed to rent a house for our outreach center. There was a two-year waiting list, and the local residents had priority. We were told that we would never be able to get a place, but God's favor said otherwise. He intervened for us, and we secured a place within three days. It was simply undeserved, unmerited favor that gave us this advantage. We were also able to easily get three more places in the next year as our ministry grew. God's favor gives advantage.

I am sure you have experienced both rejection and favor in your life, and I am confident I can predict which of these two you like better. Favor has many benefits; it opens doors of opportunities for you. It can deliver you from isolation and attract many blessings to you. In fact, favor is like a blessing magnet, and it is one of God's wonderful gifts freely given to you. He wants you to experience His favor because you are His precious daughter.

Get ready to be lavished with new levels of great favor on your life. It is in God's heart to do so for you.

DECREES

I DECREE THAT:

1. God's favor in my life is priceless, more valuable than silver or the finest gold.
2. Favor surrounds me like a shield. It covers and protects me from fear and rejection.
3. I am blessed with divine favor that causes my enemies to be at peace with me.
4. God's favor in my life increases positive influence with my family and friends and in my workplace and community.
5. Because of favor in my life, doors of opportunity are opened to me easily.
6. I continue to grow daily in favor and receive favor every place I go.
7. The favor in my life is like a cloud full of spring rain that falls on my life and drenches me like heavenly dew bringing refreshment to me each day.
8. The Lord favors me; He confirms and establishes my hands so that all I put my hands to is blessed.
9. Favor bathes my feet in butter and leads my footsteps on the right path.
10. Favor pursues me daily, giving me preferential treatment.

Decrees based on the following Scriptures: Proverbs 22:1; Psalm 5:12; 30:5, 7; Proverbs 16:17; Luke 2:52; Proverbs 16:15; 19:12; Isaiah 45:1; Psalm 45:12; 90:17; Job 29:6; Psalm 23:6; Job 5:9.

ACTIVATION

Imagine yourself walking in absolute favor. Make a list of the areas of your life where you do not experience favor, then take time to ponder, dream, and imagine those areas saturated with God's favor. What do you see? Pray for your dream to become a reality.

_____

_____

_____

_____

_____

_____

_____

_____

_____

_____

_____

_____

_____

BLESSED WITH
FEARLESSNESS

*For God will never give you the spirit of fear, but the Holy
Spirit who gives you mighty power, love, and self-control.*
2 TIMOTHY 1:7

The phrase "fear not" is found 331 times in the King James
Version of the Bible. God wants us to treat fear like a ferocious enemy.
We are to give no place to it. Fear is crippling and works in a way
similar to faith but in the negative; it could be described as "the devil's
faith." Job confirms this sobering fact concerning the power and
influence of fear in your life: "For the thing I greatly feared has come
upon me, and what I dreaded has happened to me" (Job 3:25 NKJV).

Crystal, a young woman in her mid-teens, was a contestant
in a singing competition at her school. She had a beautiful, trained
voice and was the "full package" on stage. Her passion as she sang
was electrifying, and she engaged all who were listening. The crowds
were captured by her authenticity, stage presence, gift, and charisma
as she stood among the five finalists. Her ratings were high and she
was endowed with great favor. Many believed she would win the
competition hands down.

To that point in the competition, Crystal had embraced a healthy
measure of confidence, but when she looked at the other four finalists,
she was shaken. She began to believe she was inferior, without any
right to be at this stage in the competition. Critical thoughts and
doubts regarding her talent plagued her, and night terrors of failing

with humiliating worst-case scenarios invaded her dreams. Her voice coach and parents attempted to talk her through it, but she was paralyzed with torment. Her mind fixated on the lies to the point that she withdrew from the competition. She had lost all confidence. Fear was the culprit.

Following the competition, during a counseling session, she became aware of her brutal enemy—*fear*. This enemy had stolen her potential and her dream. She had believed his lies, and now it was time to make the devil sorry he had ever tried. She continued to faithfully train her vocal abilities, but she also strengthened a strong foundation of core beliefs based on biblical truth that produced an unwavering faith that gave her courage to compete again. God had not offered her fear; He offered her strength, victory, courage, and fulfillment! He gave her the ability to do all things through Him.

Her goal wasn't about winning a competition—it was about overcoming the lies the enemy threw at her so she could become absolutely fearless. The following year she entered the competition again, and this time, once again, made it all the way to the finals. She stood against the enemy, strong in her faith, refusing to let fear steal her confidence. She won second place in the competition, but the real victory was conquering her battle over fear. It wasn't the last time she was tempted by fear and insecurity, but she had become fearless. Now she knew how to face her fears and the lies that created them. She went on to engage in a singing career with a new value of fearlessness in her life.

Don't let fear lie to you and steal your dreams and potential. You are fearless in Christ. You can face anything and win. He says so.

DECREES

I DECREE THAT:

1. I do not have a spirit of fear, but I am filled with mighty power, love, and a sound mind.
2. I am strengthened with power and might in my inner being.
3. I am of good courage and successfully face my fears.
4. I set my mind on things that are good, pure, honorable, and of an excellent report.
5. I lay hold of the truth, and the truth sets me free.
6. Like Joshua, I am fearless, strong, and of good courage.
7. I do not fear, for my heavenly Father has chosen gladly to give me the kingdom.
8. I am bold as a lion in Christ.
9. I am fully confident in the Lord.
10. In Jesus' name I cast down in my mind, every fearful thought and imagination that is raised up against the truth.

Decrees based on the following Scriptures: 2 Timothy 1:7; Ephesians 3:16; Psalm 31:24; Philippians 4:9; John 8:32; Joshua 1:7; Luke 12:32; Proverbs 28:1; 3:26; 2 Corinthians 10:5.

ACTIVATION

Identify lies in your life that have produced fear. How can you replace them with the truth based on God's Word?

_____

_____

_____

_____

_____

_____

_____

_____

_____

_____

_____

_____

_____

_____

_____

DAY SIX

BLESSED WITH WISDOM

Her teachings are filled with wisdom and kindness
as loving instruction pours from her lips.

PROVERBS 31:26

King Solomon was famous for both his wisdom and his wealth (see 1 Kings 10:1–9). Although we know that wisdom's source is God Himself, we discover in the book of Proverbs that it was actually Solomon's mother who nurtured God's wisdom into his life. For a number of years, I read the first eight to ten chapters of Proverbs every day because I longed for wisdom and knew that when we meditate on the Word day and night, we prosper (Psalm 1:1–3). I desired to be prospered in wisdom.

Women are so beautiful when they are clothed in wisdom. A wise woman exudes God's glory and beauty in profound and rich ways. I believe that is why Proverbs teaches us that wisdom's value is beyond anything in the world we could long for: "It is a more valuable commodity than gold and gemstones, for there is nothing you desire that could compare to her" (Proverbs 3:15).

Wisdom is called the "principal thing" (Proverbs 4:7 KJV). In other words, it is the foundation for many other things in your life and therefore an important focus. You may have knowledge, but if you don't have wisdom, you might not know how to communicate or apply it. You might have great amounts of money given to you, but if you lack wisdom, you could lose it. Wisdom affects every area of your life.

As women, we face many challenges throughout our day. We need wisdom to raise our families, to be a light in the workplace, and to be a representative of God's nature, light, and truth in the darkness of the world we live in. Wisdom will give us what we need to be victorious in everything we face in life.

Here is a description of the wisdom God has offered you in the New Testament: "But the wisdom from above is always pure, filled with peace, considerate and teachable. It is filled with love and never displays prejudice or hypocrisy in any form and it always bears the beautiful harvest of righteousness! Good seeds of wisdom's fruit will be planted with peaceful acts by those who cherish making peace" (James 3:17–18).

Would you like to be filled and clothed with this wonderful wisdom from God? You can be. It is a blessing He has prepared for you. Ask in faith and receive.

And if anyone longs to be wise,
ask God for wisdom and he will give it!

JAMES 1:5

DECREES

I DECREE THAT:

1. I am blessed because I have discovered wisdom, and as a result I have gained understanding.
2. I prize and embrace wisdom; therefore, wisdom exalts and honors me. It places on my head a garland of grace. Wisdom presents me with a crown of beauty.
3. I seek wisdom with all my heart, for it is more valuable than silver and hidden treasures.
4. Wisdom is a principal foundation stone in my life, and in every situation I face, I have access to wisdom.
5. I do not lack wisdom. It is always available to me. I ask God for it, and He generously grants me all the wisdom I need for every circumstance I face.
6. When I ask for wisdom, I do not doubt, therefore it is given to me generously.
7. Because I love wisdom, both riches and honor are with me, enduring wealth and righteousness.
8. I walk in the way of wisdom, and therefore I speak noble things. My mouth speaks truth in righteousness when I am empowered by wisdom.
9. Wisdom guards my thoughts, my words, and my ways.
10. I receive wisdom from heaven that is first of all pure, then peace-loving, considerate, submissive, full of mercy and good fruit, impartial and sincere.

Decrees based on the following Scriptures: Proverbs 3:13; 4:8–9; 2:4; 4:6–8; James 1:5; Proverbs 8:17–18; 8:21; 8:6; Psalm 37:30; 39:1; James 3:17.

ACTIVATION

Pursue wisdom and make it your focus today. Throughout the day, praise the Lord with thanksgiving for the wisdom He has granted you. When you approach a difficult situation, pray for wisdom and meditate on the Scripture verses that are referenced in the Decrees section. You will discover treasure!

_____

_____

_____

_____

_____

_____

_____

_____

_____

_____

_____

BLESSED TO BE A BLESSING

Every spiritual blessing in the heavenly realm has already been lavished upon us as a love gift from our wonderful heavenly Father, the Father of our Lord Jesus— all because he sees us wrapped into Christ. This is why we celebrate him with all our hearts!

EPHESIANS 1:3

It is becoming for you as God's precious daughter to live the blessed life. You were created for it! Through Christ's finished work on the cross, you have already been blessed with every spiritual blessing in the heavenly places and also with everything that you need to live a wonderful, full, and glorious life:

> Everything we could ever need for life and complete devotion to God has already been deposited in us by his divine power. For all this was lavished upon us through the rich experience of knowing him who has called us by name and invited us to come to him through a glorious manifestation of his goodness. As a result of this, he has given you magnificent promises that are beyond all price, so that through the power of these tremendous

promises you can experience partnership with
the divine nature, by which you have escaped
the corrupt desires that are of the world.
(2 Peter 1:3–4)

God has blessed you through Christ and has called you to be a blessing to others. Because you are freely blessed by God, you can freely bestow blessings on others.

We see this confirmed in the life of Abraham. God declared that Abraham would be blessed so that he could be a blessing. In fact, all the nations of the earth are blessed by him (Genesis 12:2). We also see God directing His priests to invoke blessing upon the people. He gave them power to bless His people (Numbers 6:22–26).

The Bible teaches that all believers in Jesus are His priesthood today, and that includes you. "But you are God's chosen treasure— priests who are kings, a spiritual 'nation' set apart as God's devoted ones. He called you out of darkness to experience his marvelous light, and now he claims you as his very own. He did this so that you would broadcast his glorious wonders throughout the world" (1 Peter 2:9). That means that you are called to be a blessing to those God brings into your life. What a glorious way to live your life!

When I first became aware of this as a new believer, I took every opportunity to intentionally bless. It was glorious because not only did I see joy come to others, but my own joy and fulfillment increased! It is impossible to give blessings to others and not be blessed yourself. It feels so good to live to be a blessing. To this very day, I still live to bestow blessings on others. I can bless others through a number of ways: by giving a word of encouragement or a special discourse or God's Word and promises, by offering a prayer or ministry on someone's behalf, or by giving a gift or a financial blessing. I am blessed so I can be a blessing, and so are you.

DECREES

I DECREE THAT:

1. I am created for blessing, and as a result, I am overtaken by blessings in every area of my life.

2. I am blessed in the city and blessed in the country. I am blessed coming in and blessed going out.

3. Everything I put my hand to is blessed. My family is blessed. My provision is blessed. All that pertains to me is blessed.

4. I am blessed with victory in every challenge or obstacle I face, for I am the head and not the tail. I am above and not beneath.

5. The Lord has blessed me so that I will be a blessing to others. I cheerfully and bountifully sow blessings into the lives of others, and therefore I reap blessings bountifully.

6. The Lord blesses me and keeps me. He makes His face to shine upon me and is gracious to me. He lifts up His countenance upon me and gives me peace.

7. I am blessed with every spiritual blessing in the heavenly places in Christ, and in Him have been granted everything that pertains to life and godliness.

8. Grace and peace have been multiplied to me, and I have been granted the blessings of all God's magnificent and glorious promises in Christ Jesus.

9. It is written what God has blessed, no man can curse; therefore I am blessed in the Lord and cannot be cursed.

10. I am blessed far above all I'm able to ask, think, or imagine!

Decrees based on the following Scriptures: Genesis 1:28; Deuteronomy 28:1–13; Genesis 12:2; 2 Corinthians 9:6–7; Numbers 6:22–26; Ephesians 1:3; 2 Peter 1:2–4; Numbers 23:20; Ephesians 3:20.

ACTIVATION

Consider all the ways God has blessed you and write them down. You will be amazed at how blessed you are. Thank Him for each one and then think of ways you can be a blessing to others. Write them down and then … go.

_____

_____

_____

_____

_____

_____

_____

_____

_____

_____

_____

_____

_____

BLESSED WITH A MESSAGE

All at once, the woman dropped her water jar and ran off to her village and told everyone, "Come and meet a man at the well who told me everything I've ever done! He could be the Anointed One we've been waiting for."

JOHN 4:28–29

The woman at the well was a Samaritan woman who appeared to have had a very difficult life. Jesus had disclosed to her that He knew, through divine revelation, that she had been married five times and that the man she was currently living with was not her husband. We don't know if her five husbands had divorced her or if they had all passed on—but either way, that is a lot of tragedy! We don't know if the man she was currently living with was a lover, brother, or father, but she was in a hard situation. Her life had not been a bed of roses.

God can make messages out of our messes, and that is exactly what He did for this woman. She was so excited about the encounter she had with Jesus at the well that she went and told everyone in her village about Him. After she shared this message of hope with them, they were excited: "Hearing this, the people came streaming out of the village to go see Jesus" (John 4:30).

The account in Scripture does not tell us her name, but church tradition has identified the Samaritan woman to be Photini.[5] She was the first New Testament evangelist to win a city for Christ. Her name and her message are written down in history. Some later writings also inform that Photini went on to be named as an apostle of Jesus and died as a martyr for His glory.

You have probably heard the saying, "When life gives you lemons, make lemonade." That is exactly what this lovely Samaritan woman did with her hardships. She was given a message out of her mess, that brought great glory to God! Her story brings honor to Him for all eternity. Every time people read her story in the Bible, they are filled with the understanding of God's amazing grace. From a mess to a message!

Some of my worst blunders, trying circumstances, and embarrassing situations have become my most vibrant and life-giving messages. One of my favorite messages is for the body of Christ to know abundance in God. I have preached many messages on this topic. I have also written curriculum, hosted television programs, and written books, blogs, and decrees on this subject. The message is vibrant and life changing, but it came forth from a five-year trial that was extremely difficult—a mess! Although I would not want to go through that season in my life again, I wouldn't change it for anything because the message that came forth from it has yielded so much ongoing fruit.

Are you facing a difficult situation right now? Are you drowning in a mess that you feel powerless in? Don't be discouraged. God will reveal Himself to you in new ways in the midst of the hardships, and He will turn your mess into a life-giving message.

DECREES

I DECREE THAT:

1. God works everything together for good in my life, no matter what I am going through, because I love Him and am called according to His purpose.

2. God always causes me to triumph in the battles I face, and He brings forth a message with a sweet aroma of His presence in every situation.

3. The Lord gives me beauty for ashes.

4. I am called and anointed to be a messenger of God to prepare the way before Him.

5. The Spirit of the Lord is upon me to proclaim His good message to the poor, broken, and oppressed.

6. I overcome by the blood of the Lamb and by the word of my testimony.

7. Grace is poured upon my lips to empower me to testify of the goodness of the Lord.

8. The Lord opens my mouth that I might praise Him for His goodness.

9. My lips will shout for joy because of the redemption of the Lord. I will not keep silent.

10. I will go into my world with the boldness of the Holy Spirit, proclaiming the life-giving message of the gospel of Jesus Christ.

Decrees based on the following Scriptures: Romans 8:28;
2 Corinthians 2:14; Isaiah 61:3; Matthew 11:10; Luke 4:18;
Revelation 12:11; Psalm 45:2; 51:15; 71:23; Isaiah 62:1; Mark 16:15.

ACTIVATION

Reflect on your life and note at least one difficult time you faced. Write it out and review it. Did a message come out of the mess? If so, what is the message? If not, look for the message.

_____

_____

_____

_____

_____

_____

_____

_____

_____

_____

_____

_____

_____

BLESSED WITH SUCCESS

Sitting on the riverbank we struck up a conversation with some of the women who had gathered there. One of them was Lydia, a businesswoman from the city of Thyatira who was a dealer of exquisite purple cloth and a Jewish convert.

ACTS 16:13–14

Lydia was a woman who feared the Lord. It is believed that she was a Gentile who converted to Judaism[6] and then, through Paul's preaching, came to Christ. She was also a businesswoman who sold purple fabric. Purple dye in that day was a rare commodity only purchased by the wealthy,[7] so Lydia was a woman of influence and very successful.

Like Lydia in her day, God is raising up many successful women in this hour. His desire is for all believers to succeed in everything we put our hands to when we obey His Word: "The Lord will command the blessing upon you in your barns and in all that you put your hand to, and He will bless you in the land which the Lord your God gives you" (Deuteronomy 28:8 NASB).

"Only be strong and very courageous; be careful to do according to all the law which Moses My servant commanded you; do not turn from it to the right or to the left, so that you may have success wherever you go. This book of the law shall not depart from your mouth, but you shall meditate on it day and night, so that you may be careful to do according to all that is written in it; for then you will make your way prosperous, and then you will have success (Joshua 1:7–8 NASB).

It is clear in these two Scriptures that one of the most important keys to success is to obey the Word. We know that Lydia feared the Lord, so she would have honored and obeyed His Word.

As we discovered in an earlier devotion, it was God's will from the very beginning of time to bless mankind. God proclaimed a powerful blessing over us in the very beginning: "God blessed them; and God said to them, 'Be fruitful and multiply, and fill the earth'" (Genesis 1:28 NASB).

To bless means "to invoke divine favor or care upon" and "to confer prosperity or happiness upon,"[8] or it can mean "empowered to succeed." This is great news! You are called into God's blessing, and if God has blessed you, who can curse you? To live blessed in the Lord creates the manifestation of success and fruitfulness in life. This is amazing! God invoked His blessing upon mankind immediately after He created us. That blessing gives you all the empowerment you need to succeed.

You were not created for failure; that is why it doesn't feel right when you experience it. That is why you can be emotionally jolted when the fear of failure knocks on the door of your heart. You were created to be fruitful, to multiply, and to fill the earth with His glory and goodness. Perhaps you are a businesswoman like Lydia, or perhaps you are a homemaker, a practicing professional, or a laborer in the marketplace. Whatever your walk in life, you are called to succeed in everything that pertains to your life. Jesus made the way for you, so go and succeed!

DECREES

I DECREE THAT:

1. I meditate on the Word day and night and prosper in all that I do.
2. I prosper in every aspect of my life as my soul prospers.
3. The Lord causes me to succeed everywhere I go.
4. The blessing of the Lord causes me to be fruitful.
5. I am filled with wisdom, and wisdom grants me advantage to succeed.
6. I am a doer of God's Word, and as a result I prosper in all that I engage in.
7. My relationships, assignments, spiritual growth, health, and labors all prosper in the Lord.
8. I bear much fruit because I abide in the Lord.
9. I am diligent and therefore I succeed.
10. The Lord makes the path of a successful life known to me.

Decrees based on the following Scriptures: Psalm 1:2–3; 3 John 1:2; Joshua 1:7–8; Genesis 1:28; Ecclesiastes 10:10; Deuteronomy 29:9; John 15:5; Proverbs 10:4; Psalm 16:11.

ACTIVATION

Reflect on the areas of your life in which you have already experienced success. Write them down and give thanks to God for each one. Testify to others of the success He has granted you.

_____

_____

_____

_____

_____

_____

_____

_____

_____

_____

_____

_____

BLESSED WITH STRENGTH AND VALOR

Who could ever find a wife like this one—
she is a woman of strength and mighty valor! …
She wraps herself in strength, might,
and power in all her works.

PROVERBS 31:10, 17

I had the honor of walking with a wonderful young woman of God from the time she became a new Christian. She grew beautifully in the Lord. She was strong in her core, full of courage and virtue.

One day she came to me discouraged, as someone had cruelly and carelessly accused her of being too aggressive and passionate about some justice issues she had given her attention to. She cried in my arms and said, "I don't know how to tone my passion down." My response to her was, "Let the strong be strong."

Every strength has a corresponding weakness, and although we do need to be aware of the weaknesses, God would never want us to diminish our strength, focus, and passion for the things He's called us to. He is the One who gives us strength, and He expects us to steward that strength for His glory.

My friend found her inner strength in the midst of that particular season of accusation, groomed the areas in her life that needed to be addressed, and rose up in valor to lead the troops to fight for those who were unfairly treated and who did not have a voice to protect or defend themselves. She has become a powerful leader who influences nations. It is good that she didn't back down when her strength was being challenged. Her humility in dealing with the things that needed to be dealt with in her life made her even stronger. She made the difficulties of that season work for her and not against her.

In Proverbs 31, we are introduced to this amazing virtuous woman who is a wonderful model for us all. Not only was she faithful in her home, marriage, and family, but she was also a righteous influence in the business world and generous to the poor. This woman was referred to as a woman of strength and valor who "wrapped herself in strength, might, and power in all her works." Imagine yourself being wrapped in God's strength, might, and power. What a beautiful meditation!

In Ephesians 6:10, Paul encourages believers to be strong in the Lord: "Be supernaturally infused with strength through your life-union with the Lord Jesus. Stand victorious with the force of his explosive power flowing in and through you." Paul gives believers a clear invitation in this passage to rise up and prevail in the strength of the Lord.

God has created special strengths, gifts, and abilities in each person He has given life to. When you identify those strengths in yourself and season them through testings, intentional applications, and life experience, you too will rise up like the Proverbs 31 woman. Then look forward to the following being spoken of you: "There are many valiant and noble ones, but you have ascended above them all!" (Proverbs 31:29).

DECREES

I DECREE THAT:

1. I am strong in the Lord and in the strength of His might.
2. Through Christ, I am strengthened with God's power in my inner self.
3. I am a woman filled with strength and mighty valor.
4. The Lord fills me with joy, and His joy is my strength.
5. As I wait on the Lord, I renew my strength.
6. God's wisdom, counsel, strength, and understanding live powerfully in me.
7. The Lord leads me by His power and outstretched arm.
8. I will trust and not be afraid, for the Lord is my strength and my song.
9. God is my strength and my power. He makes my way perfect.
10. God is the strength of my heart and my portion forever.

Decrees based on the following Scriptures: Ephesians 6:10; 3:16; Proverbs 31:10; Nehemiah 8:10; Isaiah 40:31; Deuteronomy 9:29; Job 12:13; Isaiah 12:2; 2 Samuel 22:33; Psalm 73:26.

ACTIVATION

Identify three areas of strength in your life, and celebrate those areas by praising and thanking God for them. Identify the corresponding weaknesses that accompany your strengths. In what ways can you refine and develop your strengths by working on the weaknesses?

_____

_____

_____

_____

_____

_____

_____

_____

_____

_____

_____

_____

BLESSED WITH FRESH REVELATION

She gives out revelation-truth to feed others.
She is like a trading ship bringing divine supplies
from the merchant.

PROVERBS 31:14

In Luke 10, Jesus and His disciples went into a village where a woman named Martha welcomed Him into her home. She had a sister living with her, Mary, who sat down at the feet of Jesus. As she attentively listened to every word He spoke, Mary received fresh revelation in His presence. Martha was very upset, as she was distracted with the dinner preparations and believed Mary should be helping her. She brought her case before Jesus: "Lord, don't you think it's unfair that my sister left me to do all the work by myself? You should tell her to get up and help me" (Luke 10:40).

The Lord's reply to her was, "Martha, my beloved Martha. Why are you upset and troubled, pulled away by all these many distractions? Are they really that important? Mary has discovered the one thing most important by choosing to sit at my feet. She is undistracted, and I won't take this privilege from her" (Luke 10:41–42).

Many things in life can distract us from the most important thing of all—time spent with the Lord in His presence, listening to His Word. In His presence, He gives fresh revelation to our hearts, and that revelation produces faith. Often I will begin to read my Bible when I don't feel motivated to read it. I just determine to separate myself from the things that distract me and focus on Him through His Word. Reading the Word might even seem dry for a while, but as I keep reading, believing in faith for revelation, it ultimately comes— the light comes on! When revelation comes, it is so exciting. It is like God Himself is right there giving understanding—and that is because He is!

God longs to bring fresh revelation to you each day, even as He opened the heavens and blessed Israel with fresh manna every day in the wilderness. There is no end to the revelation He can give you of Himself and His kingdom. The key is to position yourself in expectation for the blessing of revelation to fill your heart.

Mary made room for Him. She did not let the affairs of the day distract her from what was most important, and Jesus rewarded her. Let His words fill you. He will speak life-giving words to you every time you seek Him and every time you read His Word. He has blessed you with the ability to receive fresh revelation from Him.

DECREES

I DECREE THAT:

1. Jesus is my portion, and I promise to treasure His words within me.
2. I love the Lord my God with all my heart, soul, and might.
3. I do not let distractions keep me from the most important place—at the feet of Jesus.
4. The spirit of wisdom and revelation in the knowledge of Christ fills me daily.
5. The secret things of God are granted to me, my children, and my children's children when I receive revelation from Him.
6. Fresh manna from heaven is available to me daily.
7. I listen and the Lord speaks to me.
8. As I seek fresh revelation, I find it.
9. God's power establishes me according to the revelation of the mystery of Christ.
10. The Lord grants me each day my daily bread (revelation).

Decrees based on the following Scriptures: Psalm 119:57; Deuteronomy 6:5; Luke 10:38–42; Ephesians 1:17–19; Deuteronomy 29:29; Exodus 16:12–21; 1 Samuel 3:9; Matthew 7:7; Romans 16:25; Matthew 6:11.

ACTIVATION

Pray to the Father and invite Him by His Spirit to grant you fresh revelation of the knowledge of Christ and His kingdom. Then begin to read the Bible. Try to read an entire chapter or two and look for your fresh manna. Keep reading until you feel the Lord speak to your heart. Then write in a journal what the Lord is highlighting. Meditate on that throughout your day. Read the highlighted portion a number of times over the next few days, until it is established within you.

_____

_____

_____

_____

_____

_____

_____

_____

_____

_____

_____

DAY TWELVE

BLESSED WITH REEDEEMING GRACE

We will enhance your beauty,
encircling you with our golden reigns of love.
You will be marked with our redeeming grace.

SONG OF SONGS 1:11

Have you ever walked through a difficult and challenging season that brought forth devastation? At times like that, you might wonder if anything good can come out of such a season, but we have a sure promise from God that He will work all things together for good to those who love Him and who are called according to His purpose (Romans 8:28). He can take the worst situations and turn them into glorious testimonies. Your tests in life can produce testimonies.

Prior to coming to know the Lord as my personal Savior, Deliverer, and Healer, my life was a mess. I had made harmful choices, and the consequences of my actions were in full play. I had hurt people with my actions and I had hurt myself. I condemned myself and my heart was clothed in a garment of shame. Since I didn't love myself, it was hard for me to expect to receive love from anyone else.

The night I was born again, I did not feel worthy to have the Lord come into my life and truly doubted that He would; I felt too defiled, damaged, and broken, and could not understand why He would even be interested in coming into such a messed-up body. However, at the moment I invited Him to come into my heart and forgive my sins, He didn't hesitate for a moment. He flooded my heart with what felt like liquid love. I was amazed as I tasted the glory of His unconditional love and grace. He cleansed me and gave me new life; I knew that within. He favored me and I did not deserve it. It was undeserved, unmerited favor—it was amazing grace!

From that moment, He turned everything around for me. He healed everything that was wounded, bound up everything that was broken, and purified every part of me that was defiled. His redeeming grace changed it all. Today I am a minister of His gospel and testify of His goodness all over the world. He gave me beauty for my ashes and made all things new.

The best part about His grace is that you don't strive to obtain it. He gives His grace freely to you. Grace is indeed undeserved, unmerited favor, but it is also His divine influence upon your heart and life. He empowers you to fulfill His will without internal struggle. His redeeming grace is so beautiful, and He offers it to you right now.

No matter what situation you are facing at this time or what sinful choices you have made in the past, He is committed to turning it all around for you and granting you the treasures of darkness, the secret wealth of hidden places (Isaiah 45:3).

Look at what David declared before God after he had seduced the wife of his most loyal soldier, Uriah, then had him killed to try to keep her pregnancy a secret. This sin with Bathsheba brought great disgrace to David,[9] yet he found forgiveness and renewed grace and redemption in God: "Into your hands I now entrust my spirit. O Lord, the God of faithfulness, you have rescued and redeemed me" (Psalm 31:5).

God's beautiful and extravagant redeeming grace is available to all who need it. What an extravagant God we serve!

DECREES

I DECREE THAT:

1. By grace I have received the amazing gift of salvation through faith; it is not by my strife or works. I can walk and delight in this glorious gift every day.
2. The Lord has given me grace and glory; no good thing does He withhold from me as I walk uprightly.
3. By His grace, God has given me the treasures of darkness, the secret wealth of hidden places.
4. God makes all grace abound to me, so that always having all sufficiency in everything, I may have an abundance for every good deed.
5. Because I am beloved of God, every day I walk in grace and peace from my Father and the Lord Jesus Christ.
6. The Lord's grace is sufficient for me, and His power is perfected in my weakness.
7. I am strong in the grace that is in Christ Jesus.
8. I draw near with confidence to the throne of grace, where I receive mercy and find grace to help in my time of need.
9. God, in His grace, causes all things in my life to work together for good, as one who loves Him and who has been called according to His purpose.
10. I have been given gifts, power, and grace to fulfill my purpose and walk in the good works God prepared for me beforehand.

Decrees based on the following Scriptures: Ephesians 2:8;
Psalm 84:11; Isaiah 45:3; 2 Corinthians 9:8; Romans 1:7;
2 Corinthians 12:9; 2 Timothy 2:1; Hebrews 4:16; Romans 8:28;
Ephesians 2:10; 3:7; 4:7.

ACTIVATION

In what areas of your life do you need God's redeeming grace to manifest? Make a list of them. By faith receive His promises into those areas.

_____

_____

_____

_____

_____

_____

_____

_____

_____

_____

_____

_____

_____

BLESSED WITH THE GARMENT OF HUMILITY

In every relationship, each of you must wrap around yourself
the apron of a humble servant. Because: God resists you when
you are proud but multiplies grace and favor
when you are humble.

1 PETER 5:5

Humility is a quality of being courteously respectful of others. The behavior of humility is the opposite of behavior that is aggressive, arrogant, boastful, proud, self-absorbed, self-exalted, entitled, and vain. Rather than an attitude of "me first," humility will always be considerate and mindful of others first.

Jesus is our perfect model of humility. When I think of Jesus, I see Him wrapped in humility like one would wear a garment. Humility is beautiful. It is not weak but powerful, and every believer has the potential to manifest His life-giving humility. You too can wear it like you would wear an outer garment.

The apostle Paul testifies of Christ's life of humility before God and before man and also discloses the reward of that humility in Philippians 2:3–11:

Do nothing from selfishness or empty conceit, but with humility of mind regard one another as more important than yourselves; do not merely look out for your own personal interests, but also for the interests of others. Have this attitude in yourselves which was also in Christ Jesus, who, although He existed in the form of God, did not regard equality with God a thing to be grasped, but emptied Himself, taking the form of a bond-servant, and being made in the likeness of men. Being found in appearance as a man, He humbled Himself by becoming obedient to the point of death, even death on a cross. For this reason also, God highly exalted Him, and bestowed on Him the name which is above every name, so that at the name of Jesus every knee will bow, of those who are in heaven and on earth and under the earth. (NASB)

Jesus humbled Himself and as a result received the reward of eternal exaltation. The more you humble yourself, the more God will exalt and promote you. This is one of the many rewards of humility. Let's look at some others:

The Reward of Honor

"A man's pride will bring him low, but a humble spirit will obtain honor" (Proverbs 29:23 NASB).

The Reward of Inheritance and Land

"But the humble will inherit the land and will delight themselves in abundant prosperity" (Psalm 37:11 NASB).

The Reward of Riches

"The reward of humility and the fear of the Lord are riches, honor and life" (Proverbs 22:4 NASB).

The Reward of Greater Grace

"But He gives a greater grace. Therefore it says, "God is opposed to the proud, but gives grace to the humble" (James 4:6 NASB).

The Reward of Strength

"O Lord, You have heard the desire of the humble; You will strengthen their heart, You will incline Your ear" (Psalm 10:17 NASB).

The Reward of Justice and Instruction

"He leads the humble in justice, and He teaches the humble His way" (Psalm 25:9 NASB).

The Reward of Wisdom

"When pride comes, then comes dishonor, but with the humble is wisdom" (Proverbs 11:2 NASB).

God's garment of humility is available to you. As you clothe yourself in this beautiful attribute of Christ, you will make the world a better place—and the rewards far outweigh the sacrifice.

DECREES

I DECREE THAT:

1. I do nothing from selfish ambition or conceit, but with humility of mind I regard others as more important than myself.
2. Like Christ, I do not merely look out for my own personal interests, but also for the interests of others.
3. I humble myself before God and walk in obedience before Him.
4. I receive promotion because I humble myself before God.
5. God honors my humility as He leads me in justice and teaches me His way.
6. The Lord inclines His ear toward me to hear my desires, and He strengthens my heart because of my humility.
7. God rewards me with riches and abundant prosperity.
8. Inheritance of land is granted to me as I walk in humility.
9. God gives me greater grace because I am clothed in humility.
10. God rewards me with wisdom when I commit to embracing humility.

Decrees based on the following Scriptures: Philippians 2:3–5; Luke 1:52; Psalm 25:9; Psalm 10:17; 37:11; James 4:6; Proverbs 11:2.

ACTIVATION

Take note of the areas where you are already walking in humility before God and man. Thank God for His grace that has enabled you to do so. Then invite the Holy Spirit to convict you of any area in your life where you are walking in pride. If conviction comes, repent, invite God to forgive you, and then clothe yourself in humility in that area.

_____

_____

_____

_____

_____

_____

_____

_____

_____

_____

_____

BLESSED WITH GLORY

*"The very glory [the Father has] given to me
I have given to them."*

JOHN 17:22

One of my favorite Scriptures is Isaiah 60:1–3. Verse 1 says that the glory of the Lord has risen upon us because our light (Jesus) has come, and verse 3 declares that the glory will appear upon us.

Imagine yourself with God's glory appearing upon you: you wake up one morning, look in the mirror, and behold His stunning glory. You might be thinking, *But what does the glory look like? What is the glory?*

The glory of God is a huge topic, but to summarize, the glory of God includes:

1. All God is

For example, He is righteousness, truth, love, faithfulness, power, compassion, wisdom, beauty, and goodness.

2. All He possesses

He is the owner and possessor of all things! He owns the whole earth, all of its fullness, all it contains, and all that lives on it. He owns the cattle on a thousand hills, all the gold and silver, the wealth, the planets, the celestials, all that is in heaven, and all that is in both time and eternity.

3. All He does

God creates, heals, and delivers. He gives life, salvation, forgiveness, and cleansing. He works miracles and more.

The glory is *all* about God, and He wants you to have the appearance of Himself and the fullness of His glory on your life and in your life. You are a reflection and a revealer of His glory to the world around you.

Here are four keys to help you grow in the manifestation of God's glory in your life:

1. Believe that God is your glory and that He desires to fill you with His glory and to manifest His glory in and through your life. The same glory the Father gave the Son has been given to you through Christ's death on the cross. You will manifest in your life what you believe in your heart. Believe that God has truly given you His glory.

2. Focus on God Himself. Remember that the glory is about God. The more you know God, the more you will know His glory. Every experience in the glory is to lead you to Him. Try focusing and meditating on various attributes of His glory, one at a time.

3. Explore the Word regarding God and His glory. The Word is more than print on a page—it is living, spiritual reality. You will discover the power and reality of His glory as you study the Scriptures.

4. Rest and do not strive. God has already given you His glory, so there is no need to strive to acquire something you already have. The Spirit of God will fill you, lead you, and guide you into glory, so don't be anxious. God promised Moses and He promises you, "My presence shall go with you, and I will give you rest" (Exodus 33:14 NASB).

God has given you His glory as your portion—all that He is, all that He has, and all that He does. Arise and shine and allow His glory to appear upon you. Enjoy partaking of His glorious divine nature.

DECREES

I DECREE THAT:

1. I arise and shine because my light has come and the glory of the Lord has risen upon me.

2. In the midst of darkness that covers the earth and its people, the glory of the Lord appears upon me.

3. Jesus has given me the glory that the Father gave to Him.

4. Jesus is the glory and the lifter of my head.

5. The Lord grants me grace and glory. I receive glory and honor and peace as I do good.

6. God's glory is my rear guard, protecting me at all times.

7. I am being transformed into the same image of the Lord, from glory to glory.

8. The eyes of my heart have been enlightened, so that I may know the hope of His calling and the riches of the glory of His inheritance.

9. The God of all grace, who has called me to His eternal glory in Christ, will Himself perfect, confirm, strengthen, and establish me.

10. Momentary light affliction produces for me an eternal weight of glory far beyond all comparison.

Decrees based on the following Scriptures: Isaiah 60:1, 3; John 17:22; Psalm 3:3; 84:11; Isaiah 5:8; 2 Corinthians 3:18; John 5:44; Romans 2:10; 2 Corinthians 4:17; Ephesians 1:18; 1 Peter 5:10; 2 Corinthians 4:17.

ACTIVATION

Stand in front of a mirror and see by faith the glory of God manifest on your countenance. Decree over the image of yourself in the mirror the ten decrees listed above. Meditate on what your life will look like when you are fully manifesting the glory of God: all that He is, all that He has, and all that He does. Dream big!

_____

_____

_____

_____

_____

_____

_____

_____

_____

_____

_____

BLESSED WITH INCREASE

God himself will fill you with more.
Blessings upon blessings will be heaped upon you
and upon your children from the maker of heaven and earth,
the very God who made you!

PSALM 115:14–15

God's plan for you from the beginning of time was for you to increase in every good thing. In Genesis 1:28, He blessed mankind with the power to increase and multiply, and from that time on, throughout the Scriptures we find promise after promise regarding His desire to see His people increase.

We discover in Mark 4:8 that when we sow the Word, we will increase thirty-, sixty-, or a hundredfold. In Deuteronomy 1:11, we see a promise that proclaims we can increase one thousand times more than we are now.

Seriously imagine yourself increasing at least double in everything you possess right now: double your houses and lands, double your money in the bank, double your food, double your clothes, double your vehicles, double your friends, double your anointing, double your love for God, double your strength, double your joy, double your peace, double your love, double your patience, double your God encounters, double your understanding of Scripture, and double your giftings, talents, and abilities, to name a few.

That list is just a beginning, because you are appointed to multiply and increase. The lowest factor of multiplication is double, but God has so much more for you. He desires you to cultivate an expectation in your heart for significant increase in every area of your life.

My husband and I were reflecting on the goodness of God one day. We had been married forty-five years at the time. We remembered that when we were newly married, we had acquired a few things in life. We had just bought our first home, we owned a vehicle and some humble furnishings, and we possessed an almost empty bank account. Forty-five years later, we have increased in lands, houses, furniture, vehicles, equipment, and finances—and we own all kinds of bells and whistles. We have also increased in wisdom, love, gifts, talents, skills, anointing, revelation, favor, and everything that pertains to life and godliness. We have more than doubled in all these things. In fact, some of the blessings mentioned above have increased a hundredfold and beyond.

We discovered three important keys to securing increase in your life:

1. Sow a seed: If you are going to increase, you need to sow. You will not reap a harvest without sowing. A seed can be finances, time, friendship, service, clothing, food, material possessions, talents, and skills, to name a few. Sow intentionally into your desired harvest.

2. Faithful stewardship: Jesus taught that when you are faithful in a little, you will receive increase (Matthew 25:23). When we stewarded our finances, gifts, ministry callings, and material possessions well, we increased.

3. Expectation: When we expected increase in our lives, we received increase. When you understand that it is God's will for you to increase, it is easy to expect it because your expectation is based on God's promises. He loves when you believe Him. Stir up expectation for increase, and you will attract it.

As a woman of God, the Lord intends for you to be increased in everything that pertains to your life. Get ready to increase.

DECREES

I DECREE THAT:

1. God created me with the power to increase and multiply.

2. I sow generously, so I receive generously—in amounts that are pressed down, shaken together to make room for more, running over, and poured into my lap.

3. As I sow in good, fertile soil, my seed grows and increases, yielding a crop that produces thirty-, sixty-, and a hundredfold.

4. Because I honor the Lord with my wealth and with the best part of everything I produce, He will give me great increase.

5. I bring all my tithes into the storehouse, and the Lord in turn opens the windows of heaven for me, pouring out a blessing until it overflows.

6. The Lord will bless me and my family with great increase because I fear the Lord.

7. The Lord commands blessing on all that I put my hand to; He blesses me in the land He has placed me.

8. The Lord increases me a thousandfold more than I am, and blesses me according to His promise.

9. As I am a faithful steward of what the Lord has given me, He will reward me with increased returns and responsibility.

10. I sow bountifully and cheerfully, according to what I have purposed in my heart, so I reap bountifully.

Decrees based on the following Scriptures: Genesis 1:28;
Luke 6:38; Mark 4:8; Proverbs 3:9–10; Malachi 3:8–10;
Jeremiah 17:7–8; Psalm 115:13–14; Deuteronomy 28:8; 1:11;
Matthew 25:3; 2 Corinthians 9:6–8.

ACTIVATION

Evaluate your stewardship of the things God has blessed you with. Have you been faithful to tend to these things well? If not, it is never too late to change. Write down ways you can make adjustments and then act on them. Then choose two areas of your life where you would like to receive increase. Sow into those areas with expectation for increase.

_____

_____

_____

_____

_____

_____

_____

_____

_____

_____

_____

DAY SIXTEEN

BLESSED WITH UNCONDITIONAL LOVE

Look with wonder at the depth of the Father's marvelous love that he has lavished upon us. He has called us and made us his very own beloved children.

1 JOHN 3:1

I remember holding my firstborn son in my arms just moments after I delivered him. Never had I felt such love! Every part of my being was filled with adoration and awe for this precious life that had been entrusted to me. My son had not yet performed or exhibited any behavior that would warrant such love. I loved him because he was my son. He was so beautiful, so lovely in every way.

That was my first taste in understanding God's unconditional love for us. His love isn't based on behavior or performance. He loves us because we are His children. He loves us because love is His nature. Love is who He is. First John 4:8 teaches that God *is* Love! Love is a Person and He created you as an object of His affectionate love. Everything He does and is expresses love, because He is the source of love and He cannot act outside of love.

Everyone needs love because we were created for love and by Love. God spoke about the unfailing quality of His love through Jeremiah, saying, "I have loved you with an everlasting love; therefore I have drawn you with lovingkindness" (Jeremiah 31:3 NASB). His love for you will never end! It is steadfast and complete for all eternity.

In the book of Genesis, we see that mankind was separated from

God because of their fall into sin. As a result, we experienced guilt, shame, fear, and condemnation instead of love, but this was never God's intention or desire for us. We walked away from perfect love.

Through Christ, however, we have been restored to God and to His love. God knew that we did not have the ability to make our wrongs right. We owed such an enormous debt because of our sins that it was impossible for us to pay it back. As a result, He decided to pay the debt for us. He became man and paid the debt in full through His sinless life and His death on the cross. In exchange, He gave us His righteousness and eternal life.

What an extravagant gift of love! We didn't earn it. We don't deserve it. We simply receive Christ into our life as our Savior and Lord by faith. He did all the work to restore us to God—to restore us to Love. All we have to do is believe.

This glorious gift of reconciliation is not based on your ability to obey His commandments, your behavior, or your performance. It is based on His unconditional love for you—for us. He will *always* love you! You are His precious, beloved child and always will be. When you receive and understand this great and glorious love, it is easy to love Him in return with all your heart, mind, and strength. Bask in His glorious unconditional love and let it transform you.

DECREES

I DECREE THAT:

1. I am loved with God's perfect, everlasting love, and with lovingkindness He draws me to Himself.

2. I bask in this love, and nothing whatsoever will ever separate me from this love God has poured upon me.

3. God's love for me never fails; it is rich and forgiving, so gentle and kind.

4. God's love is over me as a banner that gives me covering and victory, leading me in the way I should go.

5. I follow after Him because He draws me with His intimate love.

6. I have been called to know this rich love that surpasses knowledge so that I am filled with His fullness.

7. I am the object of God's deepest love and affection!

8. Because of His love for me, I will never perish but will have everlasting life with Him.

9. The unconditional love of God wells up within me like fresh rain from above and overflows me with perfect peace.

10. The Lord pours His unfailing love upon me daily, and as a result I am able to love others freely.

Decrees based on the following Scriptures: Jeremiah 31:3; 1 John 3:1; Romans 8:38–39; 1 Corinthians 13:4, 7–8; Song of Solomon 1:2, 4; 2:4; Ephesians 3:18–20; John 3:16; Psalm 42:8; Luke 6:35.

ACTIVATION

Meditate on God's unconditional love for you. Listen for Him to speak His love words into your thoughts. Journal what He speaks to you. Savor those words. Believe those words.

_____

_____

_____

_____

_____

_____

_____

_____

_____

_____

_____

BLESSED WITH EXTRAVAGANT GENEROSITY

She is known by her extravagant generosity to the poor,
for she always reaches out her hands to those in need.

PROVERBS 31:20

God's heart is massively generous. He is extravagant in His love toward us and freely gives us all things. The virtuous woman in Proverbs 31 is described as one who generously manifests God's nature. As believers, we have been blessed with His generous nature. This "God-nature" lives within us, and we can unlock this beautiful treasure and demonstrate His generosity in the world we live in.

The opposite of a generous spirit is a withholding spirit. One morning after a church service, a believer whom I knew to be greatly blessed with material substance approached me and said, "I need your counsel." She explained that a friend of hers who happened to be a single mom with three young children was in need of food. The single mom apparently had no food in the house at all. I knew this mother of three, and she was doing her very best with what she had and was not spending money foolishly. She did not usually ask for help, although she often needed it with her little ones.

The woman of means asked me if I thought she should buy her some food. I wondered why she would even hesitate to do so—why would she need to ask? She explained that she didn't want the single mom to become dependent on her and perhaps set her up to ask for more food at another time. She was also concerned that the word would get out that she gave help and perhaps others would ask her for money or food too.

I was shocked! This woman lived in such opulence. She ate at the finest restaurants, shopped in high-end stores for clothing, indulged in regular pampering treatments, and had three cars in her driveway as well as recreational vehicles. She had so much while the single mom struggled every day with so little. I told her that if it was not in her heart to give, then to not do so—and she didn't.

A number of us rallied together to help the single mom. God used those who were blessed with His generous heart to support that precious woman and help her as she raised her children.

You can be the virtuous woman of Proverbs 31 who was known for her extravagant generosity, manifesting the nature of God. She always reaches out to those in need. I love that heart!

Extravagant generosity is what fills your life with joy! Look for ways to be generous. The poor are everywhere, and it is always fulfilling to give to someone in need. When you do, you are connecting to your God-nature. You can manifest extravagant generosity in many ways: the giving of finances, gifts, prayers, service, forgiveness, love, and friendship, to name a few. Allow the extravagant generous nature of God to be kindled afresh in your life and then find someone to pour it out on.

DECREES

I DECREE THAT:

1. I am known by my extravagant generosity to the poor, for I always reach out my hands to those in need.

2. I am happy and blessed because I am gracious to the poor.

3. I am gracious to those in need and confident that the Lord will repay me for this good deed; I will never want.

4. Because I look after the physical needs of others and satisfy the desire of the afflicted, my light will rise in the darkness. The Lord will continually guide me and give strength to my bones.

5. The Lord enriches me in every way so that I can be generous on every occasion, knowing that my generosity will result in thanksgiving to God.

6. I am blessed because I consider the poor. The Lord delivers and protects me in times of trouble, and I am called blessed in the land.

7. I love not only in word or talk but also in deed and truth, looking out for the needs of others and giving generously where needed.

8. Because God has richly provided for me, I will be rich in good works, generous and ready to share, storing up treasure as a good foundation for the future.

9. As I feed the hungry, and clothe, visit, and care for the needy, I am demonstrating my love for Jesus.

10. My prayers and gifts to the poor go up as a memorial offering before God.

Decrees based on the following Scriptures: Proverbs 31:20; 14:21; 22:9; 19:17; 28:27; Isaiah 58:7, 10–11; 2 Corinthians 9:11; Psalm 41:1–3; 1 John 3:16–18; 1 Timothy 6:17–19; Matthew 25:35–40; Acts 10:4.

ACTIVATION

Look for someone in need. In what ways can you manifest extravagant generosity toward them? How can you make their day a little brighter?

_____

_____

_____

_____

_____

_____

_____

_____

_____

_____

_____

_____

_____

BLESSED WITH A FORGIVING HEART

You kissed my heart with forgiveness,
in spite of all I've done.

PSALM 103:3

Forgiveness is a precious blessing that we receive from God, and it is a blessing that we in turn can give to others. God has forgiven us of a debt we could not pay, and He paid a debt that He did not owe. When we are forgiven much, God expects us to forgive others in return. In Matthew 6:12, Jesus teaches us to pray, "Forgive us of the wrongs we have done as we ourselves release forgiveness to those who have wronged us."

I am extremely grateful for the forgiveness God freely gave me when I received Christ as my Savior, as well as for every act of His ongoing forgiveness to this day. His forgiveness in my life causes me to respond by forgiving all who wrong me.

In Matthew 18:21–35, Jesus shares a teaching about forgiveness. Peter had asked how many times we are to forgive: "'Seven times?' Jesus answered, 'Not seven times, Peter, but seventy times seven times!'"

He continued to explain through a story of an unforgiving servant. A king had servants who borrowed money from the royal treasury. He decided to settle accounts with them. One of them owed him the equivalent of a billion dollars. He summoned the servant and said, "Pay me what you owe me." Unfortunately, the servant did not have the means to repay, so the king told his officials to seize him, his wife, and their children and sell them as slaves and sell all their possessions too.

The servant fell face down at his master's feet and begged for mercy. He asked for more time and promised to repay all that he owed. Upon hearing his pleas, the king had compassion on his servant, released him, and forgave his entire debt.

As soon as the servant left the king's presence, he met one of his fellow servants who owed him the equivalent of twenty thousand dollars. He seized him by the throat, choking him and demanding payment. The servant asked for more time to repay, but the servant who had been forgiven by the king showed no mercy. He threw his fellow servant into prison and demanded that he remain there until the entire debt was paid. When the king heard this news, he was enraged and threw the unforgiving servant into prison to be tortured until his own debt—the equivalent of a billion dollars—was fully paid.

Jesus used this story to share with us the importance of forgiveness. He said in verse 35, "In this same way, my heavenly Father will deal with any of you if you do not release forgiveness from your heart toward your fellow believers."

We have been blessed with forgiveness so that we can forgive others.

"For this reason I say to you, her sins,
which are many, have been forgiven, for she loved much;
but he who is forgiven little, loves little."
Luke 7:47 NASB

DECREES

I DECREE THAT:

1. I release forgiveness to those who have wronged me and fully experience my Father's forgiveness of my own sins.

2. I forgive those who have wronged me seventy times seven.

3. Because I forgive others' debts as mine have been forgiven, I am free from bondage and oppressors.

4. I love my enemies and pray for those who persecute me, because I am a child of my heavenly Father.

5. I rid myself of all bitterness, rage, and anger, forgiving others just as in Christ, God forgave me.

6. I neither judge nor condemn those who have wronged me, so I will not be judged or condemned by my Father. I forgive and am forgiven.

7. I do not take into account wrongs suffered, because my greatest aim is love.

8. I follow Jesus' example and ask my heavenly Father to forgive those who have sinned against me.

9. I will not allow a root of bitterness to spring up in my life, causing trouble and defilement.

10. I forgive and act kindly toward those who have intended harm against me, because even though they may have meant it for evil, God can always use it for good.

Decrees based on the following Scriptures: Matthew 6:14–15; 18:21–22; 32–35; 5:44–45; Ephesians 4:31–32; Matthew 7:1–2; 1 Corinthians 13:4–6; Luke 23:23; Hebrews 12:15; Genesis 50:20–21.

ACTIVATION

Take time to thank the Lord for all the sins of yours He has forgiven. Invite the Holy Spirit to show you any areas in your life where you are holding unforgiveness, and repent.

_____

_____

_____

_____

_____

_____

_____

_____

_____

_____

_____

_____

DAY NINETEEN

BLESSED WITH GLORIOUS PROVISION

I am convinced that my God will fully satisfy every need
you have, for I have seen the abundant riches revealed to me
through the Anointed One, Jesus Christ!

PHILIPPIANS 4:19

In the spring of 2018, I was blessed with an extraordinary spiritual encounter in the Treasury Room of heaven. While in deep worship, I was taken in the spirit to the entrance of a room in heaven with double doors open wide. I heard the Lord call on me to enter. Stepping over the threshold, I stood in speechless wonder. Every wall, ceiling, and floor in this room was constructed with what appeared to be pure gold that emanated pulsating life and light. The gold was so pure you could see through it. It seemed to go on forever, as I could not view the end of it. Glory filled the atmosphere!

In the center of the room stood a crimson wooden treasure chest filled with golden coins pulsating with shimmering light. There are no words to describe the glory of it all, but as beautiful and glorious as this sight was, everything paled in comparison to the One who stood in this room.

Behind and to the side of the treasure chest was Jesus Himself. Everything about Him radiated authority and created a sense of true awe in the atmosphere. His eyes were rich sapphire in color, and His face shone with a warm love-glow that filled the room. I wept as I beheld Him. There is nothing in life that compares to Him. He is the treasure! When you have found Him, you have truly found eternal treasure.

I was deeply impacted, as this encounter caused me to know more than any day previous that Jesus is the center of all life and the central focus of all that is in heaven and earth for all eternity. He is everything you need. When you have Him, you have access to everything you need. He *is* your provision. He *is* everything. Everything in life flows from Him.

In Christ, we have been blessed with glorious provision. He is the treasure everyone is seeking, and in Him all our needs are met. Paul understood this truth and wrote to the church at Philippi, "My God shall supply all your needs according to His riches in glory by Christ Jesus" (Philippians 4:19 NASB).

When we have a need, we sometimes get anxious and our mind gets focused on the provision that is required rather than on the Provider. There is no need to anxiously beg God for provision, because that would be asking for something we already have. We are taught in Scripture that we have already been blessed with every spiritual blessing in the heavenly places and we have already been given everything that pertains to life and godliness. God will meet our needs when we trust in Him.

You have access to His glorious provision every day of your life. Behold Him. Believe Him. Receive your glorious provision.

DECREES

I DECREE THAT:

1. All of the blessings of the Lord come and overtake me.
2. The Lord is my Shepherd; I will not want or have lack.
3. I seek the Lord and lack nothing.
4. No good thing does the Lord withhold from me because I walk uprightly.
5. I seek first the kingdom and His righteousness, and everything I need is added unto me.
6. He who did not spare His own Son but gave Him up for us all, will also with Him graciously give me all things.
7. God generously provides; He gives me everything I need and plenty left over to share with others.
8. My God and Father has blessed me with every spiritual blessing in the heavenly places in Christ.
9. I have access to every good and perfect gift that comes from above.
10. My God supplies all my needs according to His riches in glory.

Decrees based on the following Scriptures: Deuteronomy 28:6;
Psalm 23:1; 34:10; 84:11; Matthew 6:31; Romans 8:32;
2 Corinthians 9:8; Ephesians 1:3; James 1:17; Philippians 4:19.

ACTIVATION

Worship Jesus today as the One who is your Treasure. Praise Him for His glorious radiance and eternal power. Exalt Him as your Provider.

BLESSED AS AN INTERCESSOR

She sets her heart upon a nation and takes it as her own,
carrying it within her.
She labors there to plant the living vines.

PROVERBS 31:16

At times believers will cry out in desperation for God to "show up," but what many fail to understand is that He is actually waiting for His people to "show up." The earth has been given to us to steward. Right from Genesis 1:28, we see God giving man dominion over the earth. We see further evidence in Psalm 115:16: "The heavens belong to our God; they are his alone, but he has given us the earth and put us in charge."

Jesus explained in Matthew 16:18–19, "The truth of who I am will be the bedrock foundation on which I will build my church—my legislative assembly, and the power of death will not be able to overpower it! I will give you the keys of heaven's kingdom realm to forbid on earth that which is forbidden in heaven, and to release on earth that which is released in heaven."

God wants us to embrace His heart for the world and take our rightful place of legislative authority. To intercede means to "stand in the gap." We represent the needs of the earth before the Father, and we represent the Father's will and purpose to those on the earth. We have power through Christ as we execute His authority from heaven, establishing His will on the earth.

A new movement of intercession is coming to the church. Deep, fervent prayers of faith will give birth to a great harvest of souls. The Lord's power will sweep over entire nations and people groups. Unsaved loved ones will come into the kingdom because of the intercession made on their behalf. Even some of the vilest sinners will repent and be saved because of intercession made on their behalf. Sinners cannot pray for themselves; they need someone to stand in the gap for them, crying out day and night. There is nothing too hard for the Lord, and there is no one that Christ's blood can't cleanse.

God responds to faith. He doesn't respond to need. If He responded to need, then the poorest, most corrupt nations of the world would be filled and overflowing with His glory. Needs are not heaven's currency; faith is. People of faith can change the world. True believers standing in the gap will call down the will of heaven to manifest on the earth.

You are blessed, woman of God, with a mantle of prayer and intercession. Receive the blessing and pray. God will answer.

DECREES

I DECREE THAT:

1. I have set my heart upon this nation and take it as my own, carrying it within me. I labor to see it become a nation that honors God and is abundantly fruitful.

2. I cry out to God for the nations, standing on His promise that if we ask, surely He will give us the nations as our inheritance, and the very ends of the earth as our possession.

3. As I intercede for people and nations, I stand in the gap on their behalf so that God will act favorably toward them and save them from destruction or harm.

4. Jesus has given me the keys to the kingdom of heaven, and whatever I bind on earth shall be bound in heaven, and whatever I loose on earth shall be loosed in heaven.

5. As I agree with others in prayer, I stand on Jesus' promise that if two of us agree on earth about a petition, it shall be done for us by our Father who is in heaven.

6. As I call out for a greater manifestation of the Holy Spirit not only in my own life, but also in the church and the nations, I decree that as I ask, it is given to me, as I seek I find, and as I knock it is opened.

7. As I intercede for others, I pray, believing that anything I ask of the Father in Jesus' name, He will give it to me so that my joy will be made full.

8. I pray, as Jesus prayed, "Your kingdom come. Your will be done on earth as it is in heaven" (Luke 11:2 NKJV), knowing this is God's perfect will.

9. I pray for the peace of Jerusalem and all descendants of Abraham, that God's purposes for them will be completely

fulfilled, that the veil will be lifted and they may bow down and worship Jesus as their Savior, Lord, and King.

10. I diligently intercede, bringing petitions and thanksgiving on behalf of all those who are in authority, that we may lead a tranquil and quiet life in all godliness and dignity, knowing this is good and acceptable in the sight of our God and Savior.

Decrees based on the following Scriptures: Proverb 16:31; Psalm 2:8; Ezekiel 22:30; Psalm 106:3; Matthew 16:19; 18:19; Luke 11:10, 13; John 16:23–24; Matthew 6:10; Psalm 122:6; 2 Corinthians 3:16; Philippians 2:10–11; 1 Timothy 2:1–3.

ACTIVATION

Make a list of people you know personally who do not yet know the Lord. Pray in faith for the Lord to visit them with conviction, truth, and divine revelation.

_____

_____

_____

_____

_____

_____

_____

_____

_____

_____

_____

_____

DAY TWENTY-ONE

BLESSED WITH RIGHTEOUSNESS

*She searches out continually to possess
that which is pure and righteous.*

PROVERBS 31:13

In a world whose morals are compromised and where media invites the masses to engage in corrupt and deceptive mind-sets and ways, it is refreshing to find those who radiate righteousness and moral purity. Women in particular are being given a powerful opportunity in this hour to resist the world's standards and raise the bar.

A friend of mine is a professional model in the entertainment industry. When God called her initially, she knew that she was entering a field of corrupt morals and values, but she is determined to remain pure. Her first agent, while interviewing her, noted that she had stated in her profile that she would not model bathing suits or lingerie. This jarred him and he explained to her that she would lose a lot of money if she did not open herself to modeling those products. She replied, "I'm not doing this for the money."

Surprised by her response, he asked, "Well, then, what are you doing it for?" She answered, "I'm doing it to be an influence." He asked further questions regarding this statement and was intrigued by the conversation as she shared her passion to raise the moral bar and to influence her generation. He ended the interview by signing on as her agent, informing her that although he admired her values, she was probably going to forfeit opportunities and success in the industry as a result.

The exact opposite happened. Many favorable opportunities opened up for her. God used her to be a light in a dark place as she shared Spirit-led encouragement, prayer, and even prophetic ministry over makeup artists, models, photographers, and others who were on the set.

Doors continued to open until she was featured in some of the top fashion magazines in the industry. One day a high-level agent who had made many models famous approached her. He desired to become her agent but wanted her to compromise her standards—something he considered necessary in order for her to become successful. She absolutely refused, and of course he was shocked that she was unwilling to follow his professional advice. She took a stand for righteousness and would not allow the world's standards to dictate her value—and the Lord continued to open doors in the industry and raised her up to shine in the midst of worldly compromise.

The world needs to see examples of righteous virtue in women today. The value of women has been so depleted, but God is raising the bar. Proverbs 31:30–31 sums it up beautifully: "Charm can be misleading, and beauty is vain and so quickly fades, but this virtuous woman lives in the wonder, awe, and fear of the Lord. She will be praised throughout eternity. So go ahead and give her the credit that is due, for she has become a radiant woman, and all her loving works of righteousness deserve to be admired at the gateways of every city!"

DECREES

I DECREE THAT:

1. I am blessed because I do not walk in the counsel of the wicked, nor stand in the path of sinners; rather my delight is to follow God's Word.

2. The Lord guides me in paths of righteousness for His name's sake.

3. Above all, I am a woman who fears the Lord. I will be praised; even my works will bring praise.

4. Because I hunger and thirst for righteousness, I am blessed and will be satisfied.

5. God made Jesus, who knew no sin, to be sin on my behalf, so I have become the righteousness of God in Him.

6. I flee from the love of money and its temptations, and pursue righteousness, godliness, faith, love, perseverance, and gentleness.

7. Even when I suffer for the sake of righteousness, I am blessed. I do not fear intimidation, nor am I troubled.

8. By the grace of God, which has brought me salvation, I am able to deny all ungodliness and worldly desires and to live sensibly, righteously, and in a godly manner.

9. As one who has been brought from death to life, I offer every part of myself to God as an instrument of righteousness.

10. I walk by the Spirit and do not carry out the desires of the flesh; rather, I am controlled by the fruit of the Spirit within me—love, joy, peace, patience, kindness, goodness, faithfulness, gentleness, and self-control.

Decrees based on the following Scriptures: Psalm 1:1–2, 6; 112:6; Proverbs 31:31; Matthew 5:6; 2 Corinthians 5:21; 1 Timothy 6:10–11; 1 Peter 3:14; Titus 2:11–12; Romans 6:13; Galatians 5:18, 22.

ACTIVATION

You are called to radiate and manifest righteous virtue. Are there any areas of compromise in your life? Invite the Holy Spirit to lovingly convict you of them. Then repent (change your mind about it and turn away), receive forgiveness and cleansing, and receive by faith His garment of righteousness.

_____

_____

_____

_____

_____

_____

_____

_____

_____

_____

_____

DAY TWENTY-TWO

BLESSED WITH WEALTH

She's full of wealth and wisdom.
The price paid for her was greater than many jewels.
PROVERBS 31:10

Lydia was a wealthy, God-fearing businesswoman in the early church. She sold purple fabric, which was only affordable to the very rich (Acts 16:14). Today there are many opportunities for women, as God is blessing women entrepreneurs and business leaders. Many are being entrusted with great wealth.

Four states of increase are available to every believer in Christ. These are found in Genesis 26:12–13, which begins, "Now Isaac sowed in that land and reaped in the same year a hundredfold. And the Lord blessed him, and the man became rich, and continued to grow richer until he became very wealthy" (NASB):

1. Increase on the seed you sow into the kingdom

When you sow a financial seed in good soil, it returns with increase in the same way there is increase when you plant a natural seed in good ground.

2. Blessing

Isaac not only increased a hundredfold in the same year, but Scripture says "and the Lord blessed him." To be blessed means to be empowered to prosper and succeed.

3. Richness

Isaac not only increased and was blessed, but he also became rich. You can be blessed in an area but not necessarily be rich. For example, if I gave you one thousand dollars, you might say, "I received a blessing today of one thousand dollars." That thousand dollars, however, doesn't make you rich. When you are rich, you live in a state where all your needs are met and overflowing. Being rich is about your personal abundance. Isaac became rich and then richer.

4. Wealth

Wealth is your influence that is produced with the investment of your resources. Wealth influences the world you live in. You can have personal abundance (riches) but never be wealthy. When you are wealthy, the world around you is affected.

God is honoring His women with a promise of increase, blessing, riches, and wealth. The following is a prophetic word I received concerning this:

> Many women will obtain great wealth in this hour, as I will give them the power to make wealth and they will steward it well for my purposes. They will not love the world or the things of the world because the love of the Father is in them. They will increase in every good thing. It is their time for increase and acceleration in a level of wealth that will influence the world for my glory.

If you witness with that word, receive it! It's yours.

DECREES

I DECREE THAT:

1. God has given me the power to make wealth, which confirms His covenant.

2. The Lord makes me abound in prosperity in all that I produce.

3. The Lord will open for me His good storehouse and bless all the work of my hand.

4. I do not envy the wealth of the wicked, because the power of the wicked will be broken, but the Lord upholds the righteous.

5. I honor the Lord with my wealth, and from the first and best of all I produce, so I will experience an overflow with financial blessing.

6. I trust in the Lord and have made the Lord my hope and confidence; I am like a tree with roots that reach deep into the water so that even in times of drought, it never stops producing fruit.

7. I give, and an abundant return is given back to me—pressed down, shaken together to make room for more, running over, and poured into my lap.

8. Because I give freely, I will grow all the richer; I bring blessing to others so I will be enriched.

9. The blessing of the Lord makes me rich, and He adds no sorrow to it.

10. The Lord continually increases my wealth so that I can be generous on every occasion, knowing that my generosity will result in thanksgiving to God.

Decrees based on the following Scriptures: Deuteronomy 8:18; 28:11–12; Psalm 37:17; Proverbs 3:9–10; Jeremiah 17:7–8; Luke 6:38; Proverbs 1:24–25; 10:22; 2 Corinthians 9:11.

ACTIVATION

Meditate on Genesis 26:12–13. The wealth of Isaac began with a seed. In this next season, what are some seeds you can intentionally sow with a goal to build a realm of wealth in your life that will bless the world you live in with the knowledge of God?

_____

_____

_____

_____

_____

_____

_____

_____

_____

_____

_____

_____

_____

DAY TWENTY-THREE

BLESSED TO CONQUER

God has made us to be more than conquerors, and his
demonstrated love is our glorious victory over everything!

ROMANS 8:37

Life is full of challenges. So often there are adverse circumstances and pressures that war against our lives, but the wonderful news about our covenant in Christ is that we win in every circumstance! You are a conqueror and have been blessed by God to overcome in every situation that arises.

Romans 8:37 declares that you are *more* than a conqueror. The little story I am about to share with you will illustrate this truth.

There was an important wrestling match in which the grand prize for the conqueror was one million dollars. The wrestlers were passionately engaged in the ring, and finally one was taken down by the other. The referee held up the champion's arm, and the crowd shouted with excitement at his win. The television cameras and news reporters were in place for the big moment as the presenters came into the ring with a large four-by-eight-foot check for one million dollars. The crowd exploded with cheers. He was the conqueror and the prize belonged to him—that is, until he went home and signed the check over to his wife. He was the conqueror, but she was now more than a conqueror.

Jesus has already won the battle for us. He is the conqueror in every adverse situation, and with every aggressive enemy or horrific circumstance that will ever come against you. The battle has already been won, and He has given you all the benefits of His victory. You are *more* than a conqueror!

Here is another encouragement for you, from 2 Corinthians 2:14: "God always makes his grace visible in Christ, who includes us as partners of his endless triumph. Through our yielded lives he spreads the fragrance of the knowledge of God everywhere we go."

Let me share with you three powerful attributes found in conquerors:

1. Conquerors never quit

The saying goes, "Winners never quit and quitters never win," so stand strong in the midst of the battle and dream of your glorious victory.

2. Conquerors remain focused on the victory

If you allow the battle to become your focus, you could lose perspective and your faith will be hindered. Remain focused on the victory that Christ has prepared for you.

3. Conquerors are filled with joy

You will never find a negative, pessimistic, moaning and groaning champion. Champions are full of joy and excitement because they are winners. When you look past your adverse situation to the victory that lies beyond it, joy will fill you. In the process, it is important to choose joy whether you feel it or not.

No matter what you are facing right now, you win. Remain strong and don't waver in unbelief. God is with you, and He has made you more than a conqueror!

DECREES

I DECREE THAT:

1. I am strong and courageous, and always careful to do according to God's Word and guidance, with total confidence that I will have success wherever I go.

2. No weapon formed against me will prosper. This is my heritage as a servant of the Lord.

3. The Lord has given me authority to tread on serpents and scorpions, and over all the power of the enemy.

4. God has made me more than a conqueror, and in all things I overwhelmingly conquer through Him who loves me.

5. No temptation will overtake me because God is faithful and will not let me be tempted beyond what I can bear; He will also provide a way out so that I can endure it.

6. God always leads me in triumph in Christ.

7. The weapons of my warfare are divinely powerful for the destruction of fortresses, speculations, and every lofty thing raised up against the knowledge of God.

8. I have on the full armor of God, which enables me to stand my ground when facing evil; after I have done everything, I stand.

9. I am an overcomer because greater is He that is in me than he who is in the world.

10. Because I am born of God, I have overcome the world.

Decrees based on the following Scriptures: Joshua 1:8–9; Isaiah 54:17; Luke 19:10; Romans 8:37–38; 10:13; 2 Corinthians 2:14; 10:4–6; Ephesians 6:13; 1 John 4:4; 5:4.

ACTIVATION

What difficult—or perhaps even seemingly impossible—challenge are you facing in this season? Focus on decreeing the decrees in light of this challenge for the next several days, until you are convinced in your inner core that victory is secured.

_____

_____

_____

_____

_____

_____

_____

_____

_____

_____

_____

DAY TWENTY-FOUR

BLESSED WITH JOY

For you bring me a continual revelation of resurrection life,
the path to the bliss that brings me face-to-face with you.

PSALM 16:11

Joy is truly a blessing from God that offers strength, vitality, and a sense of well-being, and yet life can be filled with joy-robbing drudgeries that create negative and depressed mind-sets. When you lose your joy, you lose your strength and even your quality of life. As a woman, you need joy and all the benefits it offers.

Medical science has proven that joy and laughter can bring healing to the body. Often patients with incurable diseases will be treated with laughter therapy, and as a result, some have received medically documented reversals of their conditions. The Bible even teaches that a merry heart is like medicine (Proverbs 17:22).

In heaven, joy permeates the atmosphere because in the Lord's presence there is fullness of joy. Joy is also a fruit of the Holy Spirit (Galatians 5:22). When you are in the Lord's presence and when the Spirit lives in you, you have access to divine joy.

A woman whom I will call Margaret was going through an extremely difficult season in her life. Her husband had left her and her three children for another woman. Margaret had been a committed stay-at-home mom and diligent homemaker with no job training or experience in the work world. Her husband, unbeknownst to her, had not been paying the mortgage, and he left his job to move to another part of the country. She was devastated. Overnight she lost her marriage, her home, and her financial stability. As a result of the trauma, she entered into a deep depression. She tried her best to be the support that her children needed, but she was overwhelmed.

One day as she was kneeling before God and weeping in despair, she felt the tangible touch of the Lord on her back between her shoulders. Immediately she was filled with supernatural joy and gladness. It was as if she were drinking some type of "joy juice," as her entire being was filled with a sense of elation. In the presence of this holy joy, all the despair left her and hope entered. In the midst of this visitation of joy, God also gave her wisdom, insight, and perspective that set her mind in a positive and optimistic place.

A miracle took place that day in the presence of the Lord. Her circumstances did not change, but she was given a new lease on life. She had strength to move forward and face all the transitions ahead of her.

Joy is healing for the body and the soul, and it is possible to choose joy even when you don't feel it. On one occasion, I was facing a warfare situation that could easily have caused me to feel down and discouraged, but the Lord said, "Laugh." I chose to laugh. It sounded ridiculous because it was forced, but it worked. Psalm 2:4 says that God sits in the heavens and laughs at the enemy's schemes. Within moments I was supernaturally encouraged.

God's joy can strengthen and support you through any situation. In fact, it is available to you every time you reach out and receive it by faith. The next time you need some strength and encouragement, drink some "joy juice" in His presence!

She laughs with joy.

Proverbs 31:25

DECREES

I DECREE THAT:

1. The joy of the Lord is my strength.
2. I serve the Lord with joy and a glad heart for the abundance of all things.
3. I overcome the enemy with praise and shouts of joy before the Lord.
4. My heart and my flesh sing for joy to the living God.
5. Though I do not see Him now but I believe in Him, I greatly rejoice with joy inexpressible and full of glory.
6. In His presence is fullness of joy, and at His right hand are pleasures forevermore.
7. The Holy Spirit produces the fruit of His joy within me.
8. I am filled with righteousness, peace, and joy in the Holy Spirit.
9. When I face grief, it turns to joy.
10. My joyful heart is like medicine that heals me.

Decrees based on the following Scriptures: Nehemiah 8:10; Deuteronomy 28:47; Psalm 27:6; 84:2; 1 Peter 1:8; Psalm 16:11; Galatians 5:22; Romans 14:17; John 16:20; Proverbs 17:22.

ACTIVATION

Make a list of at least five things that fill your heart with joy. Meditate on them and thank the Lord for them.

_____

_____

_____

_____

_____

_____

_____

_____

_____

_____

_____

_____

_____

BLESSED WITH GOODNESS

Lord, how wonderful you are!
You have stored up so many good things for us,
like a treasure chest heaped up
and spilling over with blessings—
all for those who honor and worship you!
Everybody knows what you can do
for those who turn and hide themselves in you.

PSALM 31:19

It is easy to question God's goodness when you are walking through "the valley of the shadow of death." David understood the challenges, and yet he locked in to his belief in the goodness of God. Perhaps you can relate to the place where David often found himself:

Lord, even when your path takes me through
the valley of deepest darkness,
fear will never conquer me, for you already
have!
You remain close to me and lead me through
it all the way.
Your authority is my strength and my peace.
The comfort of your love takes away my fear.
I'll never be lonely, for you are near.

You become my delicious feast
even when my enemies dare to fight.
You anoint me with the fragrance of your
Holy Spirit;
you give me all I can drink of you until my
heart overflows.
So why would I fear the future?
For your goodness and love pursue me all the
days of my life.
Then afterward, when my life is through,
I'll return to your glorious presence to be
forever with you! (Psalm 23:4–6)

Daniela received a prophetic promise from God concerning her healing from a five-year affliction of fibromyalgia. She stood on the prophetic promise and was fully convinced through her study of Scripture that God was a healing God and that Jesus never refused to heal anyone who came to Him in faith. She was determined to keep the faith, yet daily symptoms shouted at her. The enemy would tempt her day after day with thoughts of giving up and forgetting God's Word—perhaps it was just wishful thinking.

One day as she was experiencing much discomfort and a lack of motivation to "fight the good fight of faith" (1 Timothy 6:12 NASB), a friend came by and suggested that she raise her voice in praise regarding the goodness of God. She repeated over and over, "God, you are good. God, you are good."

Her praise of the goodness of God did not last for just a few minutes but for over an hour; she kept decreeing the goodness of God in her praise. Then she was filled with hope, strength, refreshment, and determination. No matter what, she was going to believe in God's goodness in her life even as she walked through this dark season waiting for her healing to manifest. Every time she got discouraged, she would praise God for His goodness and again experience refreshment in her soul.

Over a year later, she was in a meeting where the evangelist was ministering the healing anointing. You guessed it! She was miraculously healed. Her belief and confession of the goodness of God opened the realm for her healing. She remained focused on God's goodness just like David did, and God gave her the breakthrough.

God is good all the time, and He works everything together for good to those who love Him. In every situation in life, there is opportunity to know the goodness of God. Delight in Him and believe for His goodness to manifest.

DECREES

I DECREE THAT:

1. God's goodness and mercy will follow me all the days of my life.

2. I can taste and see that the Lord is good! I am blessed because I take refuge in Him.

3. I am blessed because I dwell in His courts. I shall be satisfied with the goodness of His house.

4. I never have reason to despair, because I will see the goodness of the Lord.

5. The Lord God is a sun and shield; the Lord bestows favor and honor. No good thing does He withhold from me.

6. I continually give thanks to the Lord, for He is good, for His lovingkindness is everlasting.

7. I praise the Lord, for He is good; I sing to His name, for it is pleasant.

8. God causes all things to work for good in my life because He loves me and I am called according to His purpose.

9. God, in His goodness and divine power, has granted to me all things that pertain to life and godliness.

10. Every good and perfect gift I receive is from above.

Decrees based on the following Scriptures: Psalm 23:6; 34:8; 65:4; 27:13; 84:11; 107:1; 135:3; Romans 8:28; James 1:18.

ACTIVATION

It's time to count your blessings. What things in your life are you most thankful for? Take time today to rejoice in the Lord and praise Him for His goodness.

_____

_____

_____

_____

_____

_____

_____

_____

_____

_____

_____

_____

_____

BLESSED WITH HOPE

But those who hope in the Lord will be happy and pleased!
Our help comes from the God of Jacob!

PSALM 146:5

My father was a great influence in my life, and one of his many admirable attributes was that he was always filled with hope. He continuously instructed me to look for the silver lining in every cloud, as he was a positive man who never lost hope, no matter how serious the problem he was facing. He always had an expectation for a great outcome and actually refused to accept anything short of that. He always chose to embrace hope.

Hope is a joyful expectation for a good outcome, and it is a catalyst for breakthroughs in your life. It is a launching pad for dreams to be fulfilled. It is important to cultivate hope as you are faced with a choice to be either hopeless or hope-filled whenever you face situations that are difficult.

The world we live in is filled with hopelessness, but we are to rise up as God's ambassadors of hope. When you are filled with hope, you can help others find it in their darkest hour.

One portion of Scripture I love that speaks of the power of hope is found in Job 14:7–9: "For there is hope for a tree, when it is cut down, that it will sprout again, and its shoots will not fail. Though its roots grow old in the ground and its stump dies in the dry soil, at the scent of water it will flourish and put forth sprigs like a plant" (NASB).

I found an illustration of this in a real-life situation. I had put a plant in the garage, as I planned to put it in a larger pot, but I left it on the shelf and forgot about it. Months later, I found it. It was all shriveled up and dead. I was going to throw it in the garbage but felt that I should try resurrecting it. I brought it into the house and gave it some light and a good drink of water, then kept it hydrated. Within a number of days, it started to perk up and some new sprouts of life came up through the soil. In the next month or so, it regained its life and beauty.

Sometimes your life might feel like that dried-up plant. In the natural, it looks like it is done for, but all you probably need is a little nurture—a little hope.

> *When hope's dream seems to drag on and on,*
> *the delay can be depressing.*
> *But when at last your dream comes true,*
> *life's sweetness will satisfy your soul.*
> PROVERBS 13:12

May you always be filled with His glorious hope!

DECREES

I DECREE THAT:

1. I trust in the plans that God has for me, knowing I have a future filled with hope.
2. I am blessed because my hope is in the Lord.
3. Because I have sought wisdom, I have a future and my hope is not cut off.
4. The Lord is my portion; therefore I have hope in Him.
5. I do not lose heart, knowing my inner self is being renewed day by day even in the midst of affliction.
6. I have been born again to a living hope through the resurrection of Jesus Christ.
7. I rejoice in the hope of the glory of God, knowing that suffering produces endurance, and endurance produces character, and character produces hope, which does not put me to shame.
8. God is for me, so nothing and no one can successfully be against me; nothing can separate me from God's love.
9. The God of hope fills me with all joy and peace in believing; by the power of the Holy Spirit I abound in hope.
10. Like Abraham, in hope against hope I believe, even when God's promise has not yet manifested.

Decrees based on the following Scriptures: Jeremiah 29:11; Psalm 42:5; 146:5; Proverbs 24:14; Lamentations 3:24; 2 Corinthians 4:16–18; 1 Peter 1:3; Romans 5:2–5; 8:31, 39; 15:13; 4:18.

ACTIVATION

Who do you know who is in need of hope? Pray about gracing them with hope-filled encouragement. Become God's ambassador of hope.

_____

_____

_____

_____

_____

_____

_____

_____

_____

_____

_____

_____

_____

DAY TWENTY-SEVEN

BLESSED WITH HEAVENLY PERSPECTIVE

Yes, feast on all the treasures of the heavenly realm and fill your thoughts with heavenly realities, and not with the distractions of the natural realm.

COLOSSIANS 3:2

You have probably heard the saying, "Stop being so heavenly minded or you'll be no earthly good." That is so far from the truth! God wants us to live from a heavenly perspective just like Jesus did. In John 5:19, Jesus said, "I speak to you timeless truth. The Son is not able to do anything from himself or through my own initiative. I only do the works that I see the Father doing, for the Son does the same works as his Father."

Jesus did everything He did on the earth with a heavenly perspective. He even taught us to pray for His kingdom to come and His will to be done on earth as it is in heaven (Matthew 6:10). Once you are born again, you are no longer an earthly being trying to get into heaven; you are a heavenly being living on the earth.

Through Christ you have access to the supernatural dimension—the miracle realm. We are warned by the apostle Paul that in the last days there will be those who hold to a form of godliness but deny the power, and that we are to avoid such ones (2 Timothy 3:5). That is strong instruction, but God wants His people to be divine in nature, living with a heavenly perspective.

In my first third-heaven encounter, I heard what seemed like millions of voices in heaven laughing. At that time in my life, I had been in intense intercession. In fact, it was so intense that I had called my entire team to three forty-day fasts in the same year prior to the visitation. We were attempting to break the power of sin and corruption in the world, and the more we prayed, the worse things seemed to get. It was frustrating, so when I was taken into heaven and heard laughter, it somewhat offended me. I couldn't understand why they were all having a party and filled with joy when we were suffering on earth.

The Lord knew my struggles and said, "There is no fear, anxiety, or stress in heaven. We are in the eternal dimension living in the fullness of the victory. If you were to see as we see, you would not be anxious, fearful, or frustrated but would have assurance that righteousness and peace will be established in the earth." He further taught me through that experience that it is not my human efforts and striving that will bring the results, but my faith in what Christ accomplished.

That encounter changed my life, and it certainly changed the way I prayed. I began to teach on third-heaven intercession—praying from a third-heaven perspective—and many in the body of Christ began to see divine intervention quickly in situations they were believing for.

In Revelation 4:1, John is invited to go into heaven and see what was to come: "Then suddenly, after I wrote down these messages, I saw a heavenly portal open before me, and the same trumpet-voice I heard speaking with me at the beginning broke the silence and said, 'Ascend into this realm! I want to reveal to you what must happen after this.'"

The same invitation has been given to you. Pursue a heavenly perspective.

DECREES

I DECREE THAT:

1. My mind is set on the things above and not on the things of earth.

2. I am blessed with every spiritual blessing in the heavenly places in Christ.

3. I continually praise God for the inheritance I have through Christ—one that is imperishable and undefiled and will not fade away, reserved in heaven for me.

4. I am a co-laborer with God in bringing His kingdom to earth—that His will be done on earth as it is in heaven.

5. I am focused on storing treasures in heaven; that is where my heart is.

6. I have been given the keys of the kingdom of heaven, and whatever I bind on earth shall be bound in heaven, and whatever I loose on earth shall be loosed in heaven.

7. God has seated me with Jesus in heavenly places.

8. I join in worship with all the heavenly beings, declaring, "Worthy are you, our Lord and our God, to receive glory and honor and power, for you created all things, and by your plan they were created and exist."

9. As I am surrounded by a great a cloud of witnesses, I lay aside every encumbrance and sin and run with endurance the race that is set before me, my eyes fixed on Jesus.

10. I live as a citizen of heaven, conducting myself in a manner worthy of the gospel.

Decrees based on the following Scriptures: Colossians 3:2; Hebrews 12:2; Ephesians 1:3; 1 Peter 1:3–4; Matthew 6:10, 20–21; 16:19; Ephesians 2:6; Revelation 4:11; Hebrews 12:1; Philippians 3:20.

ACTIVATION

What situation in your life is currently challenging? Ask the Lord to reveal to you heaven's perspective. Meditate on that perspective until you have an internal conviction that there is complete agreement with it. Apply that perspective to your situation and watch your situation change.

_____

_____

_____

_____

_____

_____

_____

_____

_____

_____

_____

_____

BLESSED WITH MERCY

How satisfied you are when you demonstrate tender mercy!
For tender mercy will be demonstrated to you.

MATTHEW 5:7

Oh, the tender mercies of God are so beautiful, and they are new every morning for every believer! As sure as the sun rises each day, we can be assured that His wonderful mercies will fill our lives afresh.

Mercy is one of the blessings of salvation that I am forever grateful for. Someone told me years ago that mercy defined is "not getting what you deserve." We all deserve to pay devastating consequences for our sin, and ultimately we deserve eternal punishment, but God's mercy covers it all. Mercy has triumphed over judgment! What a relief!

Scripture teaches us that as we have received mercy, we are to share it freely with others. Individuals will often welcome mercy for their own lives and yet give so little grace to others. I have always felt a holy obligation to be merciful to others, as I need so much myself. That is one area of my life, for sure, that I don't want to withhold!

The mercy of God is so great that when we focus on it and decree it, we will see His glory. Look at what happened on the day when Solomon was dedicating the temple: "Indeed it came to pass, when the trumpeters and singers were as one, to make one sound to be heard in praising and thanking the Lord, and when they lifted up their voice with the trumpets and cymbals and instruments of music, and praised the Lord, saying: 'For He is good, for His mercy endures forever,' that the house, the house of the Lord, was filled with a cloud" (2 Chronicles 5:13 NKJV).

At the very proclamation of God's goodness as demonstrated through His mercy, His glory manifests. As I was meditating on this one day, I felt the Holy Spirit instruct me to meditate on the sweet mercies of God in my life and to decree the very proclamation the priests did in Solomon's day: "He is good, for His mercy endures forever."

Over and over I decreed this verse, and every time I made the proclamation, the revelation of His mercy became sweeter. Eventually, I felt the tangible manifest presence of the Lord fill me and surround me.

His mercy means so much to Him. It is extravagant mercy, and when we acknowledge it, He is delighted. The nature of God is full of mercy, and because we are made in His image and likeness, we are to be merciful also.

In life, you will have many opportunities to demonstrate extravagant mercy. You might think, *But they don't deserve it because they mistreated me so much. They deserve to pay big-time for what they did!* Remember what mercy is: "not getting what you deserve." In the same way you have received His extravagant mercy, pour it out on others and enter the glory. When you wear mercy, you are beautified.

DECREES

I DECREE THAT:

1. The Lord is good and His mercies endure forever in my life.
2. His mercies are new every morning.
3. The Lord is gracious and merciful. He is slow to anger and great in lovingkindness.
4. I am blessed because I am merciful; I will receive mercy.
5. The Lord will be merciful to my iniquities. He will remember my sins no more.
6. I will be merciful, just as my Father is merciful.
7. The Lord's mercy is upon generation after generation toward those who fear Him.
8. I am saved, not on the basis of my deeds but according to His mercy.
9. I can draw near with confidence to the throne of grace, so that I may receive mercy and find grace to help in my time of need.
10. The wisdom I receive from above is pure, peaceable, gentle, reasonable, and full of mercy and good fruits.

Decrees based on the following Scriptures: 2 Chronicles 5:13; Lamentations 3:22–23; Psalm 145:8; Matthew 5:7; Hebrews 8:12; Luke 6:36; 1:50; Titus 3:5; Hebrews 4:16; James 3:17.

ACTIVATION

Recall some times in your life when you were careless or you sinned. What would your life be like if you were never shown mercy? Worship the Lord for His mercy. Meditate on His mercy. Decree that He is good, for His mercy endures forever, and then look for someone who needs mercy and go pour it out on them.

_____

_____

_____

_____

_____

_____

_____

_____

_____

_____

_____

BLESSED WITH FULFILLED DESIRE

*May God give you every desire of your heart
and carry out your every plan.*

PSALM 20:4

Fulfilled desire is important in life. Proverbs 13:12 states that when hope is deferred the heart is sick, but when desire is fulfilled it is like a tree of life.

A woman whom I will call Sarah had a deep longing to be married ever since she was a young girl. Her first serious relationship was in her senior year of high school. She was in love, and she and her boyfriend talked about getting married once they finished two years of career training. Following their high school graduation, they went to colleges in different communities and only saw each other a couple of weekends a month, although they talked on the phone daily. Sarah was faithful as she eagerly awaited the day they would be officially engaged and then married.

They had almost finished their first year of college when Sarah's boyfriend informed her that he had fallen in love with someone else and he broke up with her. She was devastated—her heart was sick. That was the first heartbreak, but two more broken relationships then followed. By the time she was thirty, she had three failed relationships and each one had broken her heart. Fear entered her with tormenting lies that she would never be married and would never have her dream fulfilled. The deferred hope had made her heart sick.

She wrestled with her emotions, pain, and ongoing tormenting fear, then one day she met the true love of her life. It was unexpected, as she was simply grabbing a coffee and there he was. They connected, fell in love quickly, and within one year were married. Now they have three beautiful children.

Sarah is elated with her life. She has looked back at the failed relationships and realized that in many ways, the breakups were a blessing in disguise, as she would not have been as happy with any of those other men. Two of them married other women but eventually separated, and one of them came out of the closet as being gay. For a season her hope was deferred (note: only deferred and not destroyed), but when her desire was realized, it was a tree of life to her.

Perhaps you are in a place where some dreams are on hold. It doesn't mean that your desires will not be realized, but rather they are in the making. God will be faithful to you. As you are waiting for your breakthrough, delight yourself in the Lord. He is worthy of all your affection and desires. Pour out your worship on Him; He knows your desires and He longs to fulfill them. Give Him any anxious and fearful thoughts about your future. Trust Him. You will be so contented and overflowing with joy when you find your desire fulfilled.

Make God the utmost delight and pleasure of your life,

and he will provide for you what you desire the most.

PSALM 37:4

DECREES

I DECREE THAT:

1. I delight myself in the Lord, knowing that in due time He will give me the desires of my heart.

2. I keep myself humble, so the Lord has heard my desire. He will strengthen my heart; He will incline His ear.

3. The Lord has given me my heart's desire; He has not withheld the request of my lips.

4. The Lord opens His hands and fulfills the desire of every living thing.

5. The Lord will fulfill the desire of those who fear Him.

6. Because I have given myself to the hungry and satisfied the desire of the afflicted, the Lord will satisfy my desire in scorched places, and give strength to my bones.

7. The desire of the righteous will be granted.

8. Because I abide in the Lord and His words abide in me, I can ask whatever I wish, and it will be done for me.

9. I have confidence that He hears anything I ask for according to His will, and He will grant those requests.

10. I am anxious for nothing, for in everything by prayer and thanksgiving I let my requests be made known to God.

Decrees based on the following Scriptures: Psalm 37:4; 10:17;
145:16, 19; Isaiah 58:11–12; Proverbs 10:24; John 15:7;
1 John 5:14–15; Philippians 4:6.

ACTIVATION

What desire do you have that has not yet been fulfilled? Write it out, give that desire to God, delight in Him, and have confidence that He will bring it into fulfillment.

_____

_____

_____

_____

_____

_____

_____

_____

_____

_____

_____

_____

_____

BLESSED WITH THE HOLY SPIRIT

But I promise you this—the Holy Spirit will come upon you and you will be filled with power. And you will be my messengers to Jerusalem, throughout Judea, the distant provinces—even to the remotest places on earth!

ACTS 1:8

Jesus' disciples and followers loved and adored Him. When you are close to someone, it is hard to see them leave, but in John 14, Jesus explained to His disciples that He would be going away so that He could make a way for all to receive eternal life. He told them to not be troubled or afraid because He was going to send His Holy Spirit to help them.

He promised that through His Spirit, He would be with them: "And I will ask the Father and he will give you another Savior, the Holy Spirit of Truth, who will be to you a friend just like me—and he will never leave you. The world won't receive him because they can't see him or know him. But you will know him intimately, because he will make his home in you and will live inside you" (John 14:16–17).

After Jesus ascended into heaven, His disciples needed power to carry the assignment of advancing the kingdom. They could not do this in human power; they needed God's power. Jesus promised them in Acts 1:8 that when the Spirit came, they would be empowered to be witnesses in their local area and to the remotest parts of the earth.

For two thousand years, the gospel has been advancing through empowered believers. On the day of Pentecost, men and women were gathered together praying continuously in one accord for ten days and nights. The Spirit was poured out on both the men and women. Throughout the book of Acts you see what people empowered by the Holy Spirit could do. They preached the gospel, and worked miracles, signs, wonders, healings, deliverances, and resurrections. The same works Jesus did, they did also! This all happened because of the gift of the Holy Spirit.

Kathryn Kuhlman (1907–1976) was a famous healing evangelist who let the "rivers of living water" burst through her. She was fully devoted to the Holy Spirit and His power. Many would flood her meetings hoping for a miracle. Those who attended these meetings testified that the presence and power of the Spirit were unlike anything they had ever encountered. They called it "indescribable" and shared that crowds would wait for hours outside the meeting hall to get inside. In this atmosphere of the Holy Spirit's power, many healings and deliverances occurred. This wonderful handmaiden of the Lord, although her life here on earth has passed, has continued to bring glory to the Lord through the testimonies of the powerful miracles she ministered while on the earth. She has gone down in the archives of history as one who demonstrated the power of the Holy Spirit with integrity.

Women in this hour who are empowered by the Holy Spirit are doing exploits that glorify God just like those in the book of Acts and just like women in church history such as Kathryn Kuhlman. You are invited to be one of those women. Jesus has given you the gift of the Holy Spirit. Receive Him in fullness. He is waiting to use you.

DECREES

I DECREE THAT:

1. The Father has given me the Helper, the Holy Spirit, who abides with me and within me at all times.

2. I am filled with the Holy Spirit—the Spirit of wisdom and understanding, the Spirit of counsel and might, the Spirit of knowledge and the fear of the Lord.

3. These signs will accompany me: in Jesus' name I will cast out demons, I will speak with new tongues, and I will lay hands on the sick and they will recover.

4. The Holy Spirit teaches me all things and guides me in all truth.

5. I have received power by the Holy Spirit, who enables me to be Jesus' witness wherever I go, even unto the ends of the earth.

6. The works that Jesus did, I also do, and even greater works, because He has empowered me with His Holy Spirit.

7. Jesus has given me authority to tread over all the power of the enemy.

8. As I go forth and share the gospel, I do not speak with human wisdom but in the power of the Holy Spirit, who confirms the Word with signs and wonders.

9. I receive and put to work the supernatural gifts of the Holy Spirit—words of wisdom and knowledge, gifts of tongues and of prophecy, and gifts of supernatural faith, miracles, prophecy, and discernment.

10. Like Jesus, the Holy Spirit has anointed me to preach the gospel to the poor, to proclaim release to the captives and recovery of sight to the blind, and to set free the oppressed.

Decrees based on the following Scriptures: John 14:16–17; Isaiah 11:2; Luke 16:17–18; 14:26; 16:13; Acts 1:8; John 14:12; Luke 10:19; 1 Corinthians 2:4; Hebrews 2:4; 1 Corinthians 12:8–10; Luke 4:18.

ACTIVATION

Invite the Holy Spirit to fill you afresh. How can you take time to acknowledge and reverence Him?

BLESSED WITH ETERNAL LIFE

Those who truly believe in him
will not perish but be given eternal life.
JOHN 3:15

Eternity is a profound and complex concept for the human mind to comprehend. We relate easily to the temporal realm (the realm of time), and yet Scripture teaches us that our life in this realm is like a vapor. Before we know it, it is gone. In the realm of time, things decay and lose momentum, but the eternal realm is different.

Our life in the natural realm of time will only last perhaps eighty to one hundred years, but our life in eternity never ends. The choices we make in the realm of time determine our eternal position. For example, we know that Jesus Christ is the Savior of the world. God doesn't desire that even one would perish but that all would have eternal life with Him, but there is only one way—through Jesus. Jesus boldly stated in John 14:6 that He was the way, the truth, and the life, and that none could come to the Father but by Him. It is a bold claim, but it is true. If one does not choose the free gift of eternal life in Christ, then by default they have chosen eternal death. One way or the other, they will experience eternity.

We understand through Scripture that there are eternal rewards that believers receive when they engage in faith while on the earth. Hebrews 11:6 says, "And without faith living within us it would be impossible to please God. For we come to God in faith knowing that he is real and that he rewards the faith of those who give all their passion and strength into seeking him."

Scripture further instructs that the decisions we make in the realm of time, we will be accountable for in the eternal dimension. Matthew 12:36–37 is evidence that not only sinful actions will be judged but also idle words: "You can be sure of this: when the day of judgment comes, everyone will be held accountable for every careless word he has spoken. Your very words will be used as evidence against you, and your words will declare you either innocent or guilty."

Let's look again at Mary of Bethany as a great example of a woman who made eternal perspective her focus. In Luke 10, Mary's sister, Martha, had invited Jesus into their home. Martha was busy getting things ready for dinner while Mary sat at the feet of Jesus, listening undistracted to His words. Martha was upset with Mary and wanted Jesus to reprimand her, but Jesus pointed out that Mary had chosen well and that it would not be taken from her. Later, in John 12, we see Mary pouring expensive oil out over Jesus as she was preparing Him for His burial, even though others did not understand.

Mary had a view of eternity, and she lived her life with an eternal perspective. I love the words of a chorus I used to sing as a new believer:

> *Turn your eyes upon Jesus,*
> *Look full in His wonderful face,*
> *And the things of earth will grow strangely dim,*
> *In the light of His glory and grace.*[10]

Let's live with our gaze on Him—the giver of eternal life.

Christ's resurrection is your resurrection too. This is why we are to yearn for all that is above, for that's where Christ sits enthroned at the place of all power, honor, and authority! Yes, feast on all the treasures of the heavenly realm and fill your thoughts with heavenly realities, and not with the distractions of the natural realm. Your crucifixion with Christ has severed the tie to this life, and now your true life is hidden away in God in Christ.

COLOSSIANS 3:1–3

DECREES

I DECREE THAT:

1. Because I believe in Jesus, God's love gift, I will not perish but have everlasting life.

2. I have partaken of the living water that Jesus offered me; it has become a spring of water welling up to eternal life.

3. Jesus has given me eternal life, and no one can take it away from me. I am God's gift to Jesus, and no one can snatch me from His hand.

4. Jesus has prepared a dwelling place for me in His Father's house—and where He is, I will be also.

5. I have eternal life because I know the only true God and Jesus Christ, whom He has sent.

6. I fight the good fight of faith and take hold of the eternal life to which I have been called.

7. The God of all grace, who has called me to His eternal glory in Christ, will Himself perfect, confirm, strengthen, and establish me.

8. I will dwell with God for eternity. He will wipe every tear away, and there will no longer be any death, or mourning, or crying, or pain.

9. I will joyfully serve the Lord for eternity, constantly seeing His face.

10. Surely goodness and lovingkindness will follow me all the days of my life, and I will dwell in the house of the Lord forever.

Decrees based on the following Scriptures: John 3:16; 4:14; 10:28–30; 14:2–3; 17:3; 1 Timothy 6:12; 1 Peter 5:10; Revelation 21:3–4; 22:3–4; Psalm 23:6.

ACTIVATION

Take inventory of your life. Are you eternally focused or distracted by the affairs of this life? Are you like Martha or Mary? Which one would you like to identify with? Make decisions and actions that produce eternal rewards.

_____

_____

_____

_____

_____

_____

_____

_____

_____

_____

_____

Endnotes

1 *Merriam-Webster Online Dictionary, s.v.* "decree," accessed August 13, 2018, https://www.merriam-webster.com/dictionary/decree.

2 Dr. Brian Simmons, *The Passion Translation*, Proverbs 31 footnote "a": "Jewish legend is that King Lemuel was a pseudonym for Solomon, which would make his mother, Bathsheba."

3 *Strong's Concordance,* "G1411 – *dynamis*," BlueLetterBible.org, accessed August 13, 2018, https://www.blueletterbible.org/lang/lexicon/lexicon.cfm?t=kjv&strongs=g1411.

4 *YourDictionary, s.v.* "favor," accessed August 13, 2018, http://www.yourdictionary.com/favor?direct_search_result=yes, and *Merriam-Webster Online Dictionary, s.v.* "favor," accessed August 13, 2018, https://www.merriam-webster.com/dictionary/favor.

5 Simmons, *The Passion Translation*, John 4:30, footnote "a."

6 Simmons, *The Passion Translation*, Acts 16:14, footnote "c."

7 Simmons, *The Passion Translation*, Acts 16:14, footnote "b."

8 *Dictionary.com, s.v.* "bless," accessed August 31, 2018, https://www.dictionary.com/browse/bless?s=t; *Merriam-Webster, s.v.* "bless," accessed August 31, 2018, https://www.merriam-webster.com/dictionary/bless.

9 Simmons, *The Passion Translation*, Psalm 31, footnote "a."

10 Helen Howarth Lemmel, "Turn Your Eyes Upon Jesus," 1918.

ABOUT THE AUTHOR

Patricia King has been a pioneering voice in Christian ministry for more than forty years. She is a respected apostolic minister of the gospel, successful business owner, and an inventive entrepreneur. She is an accomplished itinerant speaker, author, television host, media producer, and ministry network overseer who has given her life fully to Jesus Christ and to His kingdom's advancement on the earth. She is the founder and leader of Patricia King Ministries and co-founder of XPmedia.com. You can also connect with Patricia through her social media feeds on Facebook and Twitter.